THE LAST GREAT
BATTLE OF THE SOMME

In our heart of hearts believing
Victory crowns the just,
And that braggarts must
Surely bite the dust,
Press we to the field ungrieving,
In our heart of hearts believing
Victory crowns the just.

THOMAS HARDY, 5 SEPTEMBER 1914

THE LAST GREAT
BATTLE OF THE SOMME
Beaumont Hamel 1916

G.Y. CHEYNE

JOHN DONALD PUBLISHERS LTD
EDINBURGH

To the memory of A.C.,
who was there.

© G.Y. Cheyne, 1988

ISBN 0 85976 216 5

Distributed in the United States of
America by Humanities Press Inc.,
Atlantic Highlands, NJ 07716, USA.

Phototypeset by Newtext Composition Ltd., Glasgow.
Printed in Great Britain by Bell & Bain Ltd, Glasgow.

Acknowledgements

The 'brilliant storm of Beaumont Hamel' – the phrase is Churchill's – has been largely ignored in recent accounts of the fighting on the Somme, yet the *Official History* (Macmillan, 1938), on which all who write about the War must heavily depend, provided a long and highly detailed description of the battle. That account was based chiefly upon the day-by-day entries in the War Diaries of the participating battalions; and these Diaries – fascinating records of history in the making – together with other important documentary material from the period, can be consulted at the Public Record Office, Kew. My description of the battle owes much to the anonymous writers of these Battalion Diaries.

The History of the 51st (Highland) Division, 1914-1918 by F.W. Bewsher (Blackwood, 1921) gives a lively picture of the early days of the Division at Bedford, and goes on to discuss each of the Division's subsequent battles in detail. Bewsher's book, long out of print, is obtainable now only in the larger public libraries. It is a mine of authoritative information, containing much useful material not available elsewhere.

Cyril Falls' *History of the Gordon Highlanders 1914-1919* (Aberdeen University Press, 1958) describes the important part played by the four battalions of Gordons that were present at Beaumont Hamel in 1916. A copy of P.D. Thomson's *The Gordon Highlanders* (Swiss and Co., 1920) can occasionally be found in a second-hand bookshop; it too includes a very readable account of the Gordons' experiences at Beaumont Hamel. Interesting, though not wholly reliable, descriptions of the battle appeared in contemporary issues of the *Scotsman*, the *Aberdeen Daily Journal*, and the *Times*.

For a vivid picture of the battlefield on 13 November, 1916, with its confusion and tension, there is nothing to compare with the eyewitness account given by Paul Maze in his remarkable book *A Frenchman in Khaki* (Heinemann, 1934).

I acknowledge my indebtedness to all these sources.

In compiling the chapters relating to the means of war, too many works have been consulted to be mentioned individually here; some of the most useful are listed at the end of this book under 'Further Reading'. My indebtedness to the authors of all these works is very great.

The illustration of the Memorial to the 51st (Highland) Division at Beaumont Hamel is reproduced by courtesy of the Commonwealth War Graves Commission. That of the officers of the 5th Gordon Highlanders is from a photograph in the author's possession. All the other illustrations, chosen less on their photographic merit than on their relevance to the text, are reproduced by courtesy of the Imperial War Museum; several of them have not, so far as I can establish, been published previously. I am indebted to the staff of the Museum's Department of Photographs for their assistance in making this selection.

Lastly, I wish to thank a very old soldier and scholar, Mr. A.W. Bannerman of Edinburgh, who was able to put me right on various matters, some tactical and some syntactical. Any errors that remain in my text are certainly not his responsibility.

G.Y. Cheyne
Peebles, 1988

Contents

Introduction

Between 1 July and 18 November, 1916, was fought on the Western Front the series of battles now collectively known to history as the Battle of the Somme.

On 1 July, a day of cloudless skies and uninterrupted sunshine, hopes ran high in the British camp as the men climbed out of their trenches and set off across No-Man's-Land, confident of an easy victory.

On 18 November, in contrast, the morning dawned dark and chill, with flurries of damp snow sweeping in from the north-west. The mood, too, had changed. Gone was the false optimism, the expectation of a swift victory by means of one stunning, knock-out blow. A hard lesson had been learned; no British army had ever learned a harder. Since 'The Big Push' started, 50,000 British soldiers had perished, and nearly eight times that number had been wounded.

Moreover it seemed as though little had been achieved. Some of the objectives set for the first day of the offensive – Serre, Grandcourt, Miraumont Ridge – were still in German hands at the end of the battle, 140 days later. At that rate of progress, said pessimists back home, the War would last forever, or end only when all the young men of the Empire had been slaughtered.

Yet the mood in the British lines that bleak November morning was not, as might have been expected, one of doubt and misgiving. Despite all the hardships and sacrifices and disappointments of the past four and a half months, the armies of the Empire now faced the future with growing hope and ever-increasing confidence.

The reason was not far to seek. These were men of the New Army, men from the greatly expanded Territorial battalions, and men from the farthest corners of the Empire – Canadians, Australians, New Zealanders, Indians, and South

Africans. Two years earlier most of them had been civilians with no more than a passing interest in military affairs. Then the War came, and they had flocked to the recruiting halls in their hundreds of thousands. For many months thereafter they had marched, and drilled, and tried to master the basic skills of soldiering. They had established strong friendships, and acquired pride in their parent regiments; but one all-important question had been left unanswered: how would they perform against the enemy in battle?

Now, here on the Somme, the answer to that question had been given. They had played the leading part in the greatest battle in history, and had emerged with honour. Having dared to challenge the world's strongest army, they had driven it from some of its most secure positions, and withstood more than three hundred savage counter-attacks.

Perhaps 'The Big Push' had failed to provide the strategic success which the Politicians had predicted; but the men in the trenches knew little of strategy, and had their own views on Politicians. What they did know was that they had met the enemy on equal terms and more than held their own. The Germans were old hands at the game, the British mere beginners by comparison – but learning fast. Next year, when the struggle was renewed, the British would have more men, and more guns, and tanks in their hundreds. The final outcome was no longer in doubt.

It has long been fashionable to portray the Somme as an unrelieved disaster from start to finish. 'Idealism perished on the Somme', cried one writer, adding that 'the enthusiastic volunteers were enthusiastic no longer. They had lost faith in their cause, in their leaders, in everything except loyalty to their fighting comrades' (A.J.P. Taylor, *The First World War*, Hamish Hamilton, 1963). Commentators refer to the battle as 'the graveyard of the flower of British manhood', while others go so far as to assert that 'a whole generation' had been destroyed there.

Such claims were perhaps excusable when made by those who themselves had suffered bereavement. Today, seventy years after the event, a calmer, more objective assessment is possible. It remains beyond dispute that the Somme was a tragedy and its casualties appalling. No-one who reads the balanced, dispassionate account in the *Official History* can escape being sickened by the waste of whole battalions in repeated, futile attacks on near-impregnable positions. There was muddle, incompetence, and dangerous self-deception, especially at the higher levels of command; and the victims, always, were the ordinary fighting soldiers. But there were undoubtedly other instances, too often left unmentioned even in recent accounts of the fighting, of careful planning, clever tactics, and brilliant improvisation. Surely these need not be forgotten, or glossed over, simply because they were, unhappily, the exception rather than the rule?

Nor should the first day of the Somme be given undue prominence. The huge loss of life among the British on that perfect summer morning seventy years ago has haunted later generations – understandably so; but it has to be remembered that the battle continued for nearly five more months, and in that space of time the fate of the German army was virtually sealed and the outcome of the War decided.

For the Somme was a major turning-point. Until then the issue had hung in the balance; but by the end of November the ordinary German soldier realised that victory had slipped from his grasp, and the ordinary British soldier was convinced that he could now win.

Of all that happened between July and November, 1916, nothing was more significant than this growth of confidence in the men who only two years earlier had been civilians. Upon their shoulders was to fall more and more heavily the burden of the fighting in the years ahead. It was they who would endure the agony of Passchendaele in 1917, and the ferocity of the desperate German offensives of 1918. It was they who finally broke the German war machine and led the Allies to victory. On the Somme they demonstrated the traditional military virtues of endurance, stoicism, and selfless disregard for danger; but there also they revealed an unexpected and welcome ability to learn and to adapt to the new technology of war: an ability too often lacking in their colleagues of the old professional Army.

From that legion of men who fought on the Somme, soon not one single survivor will remain. Fortunately for us, and for posterity, they will leave behind them a vast repository of first-hand evidence: diaries, reminiscences, letters, poems, commentaries, histories, and volumes of historical fiction. Some of these are works of such obvious merit or general interest that their continued publication is assured. But other works, of a more technical nature, are already difficult for the general reader to obtain; and without some understanding of the technology of the period it becomes hard to see why the War took its particular course.

For above all the Great War was one of technical change and tactical experimentation. The infantry extended their armoury to include light machine-guns, rifle grenades, and trench mortars. The artillery developed guns of increased range, power, and accuracy, employing them in numbers undreamt of in previous campaigns. The 'creeping' barrage made its appearance, as did sound-ranging, flash-spotting, and 'predicted' fire. Poison gas was used for the first time on the battlefield, and soon became a standard weapon of attack. The tank was invented. Aeroplanes mapped the ground defences, and aerial bombing and trench-strafing were introduced. Wireless attempted to solve the problem of battlefield communications. Each innovation filled a particular need, and the story of their development forms the larger part of this book.

By 1916 most of these new developments had made their appearance, and all the elements came together in the greatest battle of the War, the Battle of the Somme. There also, making their long-awaited début, were the men of Britain's great new Civilian Armies. We conclude this book with a description of their two dramatic attempts – the first ending in failure, the second in success – to storm the fortress of Beaumont Hamel, the significance of that curiously neglected last Somme battle forming the subject of our final chapter.

CHAPTER 1

Prelude to the Somme

On 15 September, 1914, Field-Marshal Sir John French, Commander-in-Chief of the British Expeditionary Force, issued an Operation Order containing the following words:

> The Commander-in-Chief wishes the line now held by the Army to be strongly entrenched, and it is his intention to assume a general offensive at the first opportunity.

Few could have guessed at the time how completely this short sentence expressed the two ideas that were to dominate British military thinking for the rest of the War: defence by means of entrenchment, and the constant hope of a decisive breakthrough.

Within a month, from the Channel to the Vosges, the front line had stiffened into a form so rigid that it remained almost intact until the huge offensives of 1918. Yet such 'static' warfare was very far from the minds of the generals – British, French, or German – when the fighting began. Indeed, for the first six weeks the War was one of rapid and continual movement.

Germany in 1914 saw her main antagonists as France and Russia. She planned to subdue her western neighbour, France, before the giant but slow-moving armies of Russia could be mobilised on her eastern border. The Schlieffen Plan, drawn up with meticulous attention to detail by a former Chief of the German General Staff, described the best route by which a decisive blow could be delivered against France. That route lay through Belgium, whose neutrality Britain had undertaken to uphold. On the morning of 4 August, 1914, two divisions of German cavalry rode across the Belgian frontier, and by midnight of the same day Britain found herself unavoidably drawn into the conflict.

One of the Krupp-built 42-cm siege cannons used by the Germans to bombard the forts around Liège and Namur in August 1914. Specially constructed vehicles hauled the monster howitzers across the German border and into position. The fall of the Belgian fortresses opened the way for a German advance on Paris.

The Schlieffen Plan provided for a broad advance through Belgium and northern France, followed by a wide left wheel encircling Paris and then taking the French frontier troops in the rear. By 20 August Liège had fallen, Brussels was about to be taken, and Namur, the last Belgian fortress on the road to Paris, was under attack.

The British Expeditionary Force completed its assembly near Le Cateau, close to the French border with Belgium, on that same day. Along with its four infantry divisions, one cavalry division, and one cavalry brigade, were four squadrons of the Royal Flying Corps – sixty-three aeroplanes in all. Significantly, a cavalry patrol on 20 August found nothing to report, but an observer on a reconnaissance flight saw the huge columns of von Kluck's First Army pressing on towards Antwerp. Already the new arm was proving the old an anachronism.

On 22 August the British encountered the Germans head-

Sir John French, first Commander-in-Chief of the British Expeditionary Force, landing at Boulogne ten days after the outbreak of war. By August 20, 100,000 British troops had crossed the Channel and – unknown to the Germans – were assembling near Mons.

on at Mons, just across the Franco-Belgian border. Two British divisions faced six German divisions, but so rapid and effective was the rifle-fire of the British Regular soldiers that German casualties were twice or thrice those of their opponents. In an often-quoted German account appears the statement that 'over every bush, hedge, and fragment of wall floated a thin film of smoke betraying a machine-gun rattling out bullets'. Such skill in musketry – for it was not British machine-guns but rifles that were responsible – was never matched by the recruits drafted later in the War.

Threatened with encirclement, the hard-pressed B.E.F. eventually fell back, together with their French allies, in the memorable 'Retreat from Mons'. At Le Cateau on 26 August a confused action left the British badly mauled but still full of fight.

It was now that the German Commander-in-Chief, General von Moltke, set in train a series of modifications to the

Fig. 1

Schlieffen Plan that were to prove fatal to German hopes of a swift decision in the West. The right of the German line, already weakened by the removal of seven divisions to mop up resistance in Belgium and the border region, was further reduced in strength by the transfer of four of its divisions to East Prussia to counter a Russian offensive there. The transfer was justified by the belief – over-optimistic as it turned out – that victory over the British and French had been as good as won. Next, in response to a request from the commander of the German Second Army, von Kluck's First Army abandoned its drive west and turned eastward to help its neighbour. This change of direction, again detected first from the air, left the right flank of the First Army

An early B.E.2. of No.2 Squadron, Royal Flying Corps, at Montrose in 1913. A similar machine made the Royal Flying Corps' first operational flight on 19 August, 1914. Despite getting lost, the pilot on that occasion eventually landed safely and was able to submit a useful report.

dangerously exposed – a situation which Galliéni, the Paris military governor, was quick to seize upon and exploit.

Galliéni induced Joffre, the French Commander-in-Chief, to halt the retreat south and strike hard at the exposed German flank. Von Kluck immediately turned towards Paris to deal with this threat, and a gap of thirty miles opened up between his army and the German Second Army. Into this gap, not without misgivings on the part of Sir John French, its volatile commander, marched the weary but undaunted B.E.F.

Rumours began to run like lightning through the German armies, now close to exhaustion after their stupendous efforts of the past month. The German Second Army decided to retreat, though indeed the threat they faced from the B.E.F. was largely illusory. This proved to be the turning point. The other German armies, infected by groundless fears and doubts, followed suit. The ensuing battle came to be known as 'the Miracle of the Marne', and to many Allied observers the retreat of the German armies after their recent overwhelming successes seemed little less than miraculous.

But in fact twenty-seven Allied divisions faced a mere thirteen German divisions on the crucial sector. Had Schlieffen's original concept not been tampered with, and the German right wing depleted of so many divisions, the outcome might have been very different.

As it was, the Allies failed also to secure a decisive victory, chiefly because their cavalry always arrived just too late to bring about an effective breakthrough.

On 14 September the Germans dug themselves into prepared positions north of the river Aisne, and the next day Sir John French issued his Operation Order for his own troops to do the same: trench warfare had arrived. The next month saw a last brief flurry of movement as each side tried to turn the other's northern flank – the so-called 'Race to the Sea' – but thereafter very large-scale maps would be needed to show the alterations in the front lines from one week to the next.

One name on the map that was to bulk tragically large for the remainder of the War was Ypres. There the Allied troops were defending a salient – a bulge – some five or six miles deep and ten miles across, around that historic Flemish cathedral city. The disadvantage of a salient, to defenders within it, is that they are exposed to enemy artillery firing at them from every direction except their rear. At Ypres the salient was further characterised by the fact that its perimeter lay mainly on higher ground: whoever held that rim of low hills held the key to the situation.

The ferocity of the German attacks was matched by the stubbornness of the defenders. As the weather deteriorated with the approach of winter, the now familiar picture developed for the first time of a tortured, shell-torn landscape in which half-frozen men stood knee-deep in waterlogged trenches, while limbers bringing up rations and ammunition sank to their axles in mud.

The battle of 'First Ypres' ground to a halt in mid-November, but thereafter, as the *Official History* puts it, 'Ypres itself was fired on daily, as if in revenge for the great

German failure with which its name will be forever associated'.

1915 saw the failure of two schemes, one British and strategic, the other German and tactical, for circumventing the stalemate on the Western Front.

The British scheme was the ill-fated Dardanelles Expedition, which sought to reduce the pressures on Russia by knocking out Turkey, Germany's partner in the eastern Mediterranean; Germany could then be attacked 'by the back door'. Hasty planning, inadequate provision of men and materials, failure to seize opportunities that arose once only and were never repeated, and above all an unexpectedly determined opponent, resulted in the ignominious withdrawal of the Expedition after eight costly months. Yet the Dardanelles adventure was close to success on more than one occasion. Had it achieved its object, the subsequent history of Russia, and thus the fate of our troubled modern world, might well have been very different.

The Germans, equally anxious for some resolution of the deadlock, turned to a tactical weapon: poison gas. When first used, at Ypres on 22 April, this terrifying novelty created a four-mile-wide breach in the Allied line; but no German reserves were available to profit from the situation, and a magnificently heroic stand by Canadian troops flanking the gap enabled the line to be restored. At the end of the Second Battle of Ypres the salient was still in Allied hands: more cramped than before, and as vulnerable as ever to the artillery ranged around it, but with neither side ready to concede defeat.

At the Chantilly Conference in December, 1915, the Allied Commanders met to decide future policy. Britain now had thirty-six divisions in France, and her military strength in weapons and ammunition was growing daily; but the new divisions were in many instances untried troops. Haig, who had succeeded French after the costly failure in September of the Battle of Loos, thought that they might be ready for large-scale operations by August, 1916. Eventually it was decided that joint offensives by all the Allies should be undertaken simultaneously, so as to split the forces of the enemy; but Verdun changed everything.

Falkenhayn, who was now the German Commander-in-Chief – Moltke having retired from the scene after the *débâcle* of the Marne – had long recognised that Britain and her Empire would become his chief antagonist if the War lasted long enough. He determined on bringing France to submission first, thereby 'knocking England's best sword out of her hand'. His decision to attack the citadel of Verdun was taken chiefly because of the psychological effect which its threatened loss would have on France: to defend Verdun he knew that France would be prepared to bleed to death. Already, by the end of 1915, France had lost over one million men on the Western Front. At Verdun Falkenhayn now hoped to deliver the *coup de grâce*.

And he almost succeeded. The German bombardment began on 21 February along a fifteen mile front. By the end of March the defenders had lost 89,000 men; three months later that total had risen to 315,000. France was brought to the very limit of her endurance. No longer could she be expected to play a major part in the summer offensive; instead, an immediate British offensive was essential to divert pressure from Verdun.

Reluctantly, but deeply conscious of France's peril, Haig agreed to fight before he was ready, on ground not of his own choosing, and on a greatly extended front. It was no recipe for success. Yet the fact remains that because of the British offensive on the Somme, Verdun held firm, the German grip upon it was forced to relax, and France herself survived.

Haig's critics condemn his conduct of the battle chiefly because he allowed it to become a battle of attrition – that is, one in which casualties are accepted, in the hope that the enemy will break first. Haig's champions point to other great battles – Ticonderoga, Bunker Hill, Albuera, Badajoz, Waterloo – where casualties were as high proportionately, though less in scale (John Terraine, *Douglas Haig, The*

Educated Soldier, Hutchinson, 1963). Perhaps in the judgement of time Haig's own assessment, made three days after the epic struggle ended, will be seen as most consistent with the facts:

> It is true that the amount of ground gained is not great. That is nothing. The strength of the defences overcome and the effect on the defenders are the real tests. Time after time in the last five months the Allies have driven the enemy, with heavy loss, from the strongest fortifications that his ingenuity could conceive and his unwearying labour could construct. Time and again his counter-attacks have been utterly defeated . . . The full value of these results will become evident in the future.

CHAPTER 2

Kitchener's Men

The British army that went to war in August, 1914 was arguably the best organised, the best trained, and the best equipped which this country ever put in the field. Whether it was also the best led is more doubtful; that it was too small to be really effective is beyond dispute.

The Expeditionary Force under Sir John French set off with just four infantry divisions and one augmented division of cavalry: 'a tiny drop in the great tides of armed might that were now in full flow' (John Terraine, *The First World War*, Papermac, 1984). On the Continent a German army one and a half million strong confronted a French army of one million and a Belgian force of one hundred and seventeen thousand. The British Expeditionary Force, a mere hundred thousand men, was so diminutive in comparison that the French chose to ignore it in their calculations.

Yet before the year closed, that same small force had secured for itself a place in history. Many of its young soldiers, who alongside the French and Belgian armies had stemmed and then turned the German tide, found graves in the carnage that was 'First Ypres'; but the influence which they exerted on their successors was incalculable. Over the years that followed, the fact that Britain's 'New Armies' proved equal to their great task was in no small measure due to the extraordinary example of efficiency, courage, and discipline set by that first 'contemptible little army' in the crucial autumn months of 1914.

What accounted for the excellence of its performance? To begin with, it was an army of professionals; of men who had chosen soldiering as their career, whose lives were indissolubly linked with the fortunes of their Regiment, and who lived – and were prepared if need be to die – for the

A famous gun, now in the Imperial War Museum, London. On 1 September, 1914, during the Retreat from Mons, this 13-pounder engaged twelve German guns at point-blank range. Capt. E.K. Bradbury (killed during the battle) and the two men who manned the gun with him were each awarded the Victoria Cross.

glory they could win for it. Let one man, Captain Francis Grenfell, speak for many:

> 15th August. We entrain today at 1 p.m. and hope to reach France tonight. We leave very quietly as if marching to manoeuvres, but a more magnificent regiment never moved out of barracks for war. Everyone is full of enthusiasm . . . So far I have been the luckiest man alive. I have had the happiest possible life, and have always been working for war, and have just got into the biggest in the prime of life for a soldier.

That is the authentic voice of the period. If it sounds strange to modern ears, as much for its exulting acceptance of duty and possible sacrifice as for its apparent absence of scruples concerning the cruel necessities of war, we need only remind ourselves, as every student of history must, that 'the past is a foreign country: they do things differently there'.

Nine days after landing in France, Grenfell won the Victoria Cross for rescuing guns under heavy fire. He was killed in action in May, 1915.

The Army of 1914 was marvellously well adapted to the fast-moving, open warfare which characterised those first weeks. Skills acquired fighting the Boers in the wide spaces of the South African veldt re-emerged to baffle and confuse the new enemy. Time and again the British would surprise a German column with murderous blasts of rifle-fire, vanish into thin air before the enemy's artillery could effectively retaliate, and then strike again from some different, quite unexpected quarter.

But this type of fighting, which was simply skirmishing on a grand scale, tested skills and strengths very different from those needed for trench warfare. Tactics which served at Mons were irrelevant at First Ypres. The Army had to change, and had to change rapidly.

Trench warfare demanded, above all, the deployment of men in numbers far exceeding anything envisaged by the military Establishment in Britain. Not until 1916 did Britain and her Empire, with a vastly larger total population than that of France, have in Europe forces comparable with those which her ally had mobilised from the very start of hostilities. For almost two years France was obliged to bear the overwhelmingly heavier share of the burden, so that when the Battle of the Somme began she had already lost, in dead and missing, more than one million of her young men.

There was one person in Britain who not only foresaw the probable length of the struggle but seems to have realised almost immediately the size of army that Britain would need to raise. Lord Kitchener, hero of minor campaigns in Egypt and the Sudan, and the man who forced defeat on the Boers in 1902, was appointed Secretary for War on the third day of hostilities, and he at once set about expanding the Army to no fewer than *seventy* divisions. He predicted that this great 'New Army' would not reach its full military capability until the third year of the War; and that by then the armies of the enemy would be on the decline. His prescience extended far into the future: 'I have no fear about winning the War,' he stated; 'I fear very much we may not make a good peace'.

Kitchener died when the cruiser *Hampshire*, taking him on an official visit to Russia, struck a mine and sank near Scapa Flow on 5 June, 1916. That same day, the last of hiˢ New Army divisions was crossing the Channel to France.

The principal formations in the Army structure merit here a brief description.

In 1914 each infantry division, totalling some 18,000 officers and men, and commanded by a major-general, was organised into three brigades, each with four battalions. Battalions were subdivided into four companies, each with four platoons, and each platoon had, as a rule, four sections. The section was the smallest unit that could function as an entity: it consisted of six to nine men and a corporal or lance-corporal. Platoons were in the charge of a platoon sergeant and led by the lowest-ranking commissioned officer, a second-lieutenant. The commander of a company was usually a captain; his non-commissioned officer was the company sergeant-major. The whole battalion was led by a lieutenant-colonel (the Commanding Officer, or 'C.O.') who had a major as his second-in-command. The Regimental Sergeant-Major was the senior non-commissioned officer in the battalion. An important officer at Battalion Headquarters was the Adjutant, whose special talent lay in coping with mountains of paperwork. By the end of the Battle of the Somme most battalions included in their headquarters establishment a Lewis-gun officer, a signals officer, a bombing officer, and an intelligence officer. The battalion doctor and the padre were attached to, but not an integral part of, the battalion.

Most infantry battalions could count on remaining with the same brigade and division for long periods, but inevitably there were exceptions. It was always a sad day when a division was split up, for its constituent battalions had usually been in battle together and shared many memories.

An issue of rum to men of the 8th Black Watch after their capture of Longueval, one of the Somme strongholds, on 14 July, 1916. The 9th (Scottish) Division suffered over 1000 casualties in that battle.

In addition to its infantry, each division in 1914 had three brigades of field artillery (fifty-four 18-pounder guns), one field howitzer brigade (eighteen 4.5-inch howitzers), and one heavy artillery battery (four 60-pounders): a total of some 4000 officers and men. There was also an ammunition column, two field companies of Royal Engineers, a Signal Company, and three field ambulance units. Not part of the division, but essential for the smooth running of the military machine, were the 'lines of communication' units – railway maintenance workers, butchers, bakers, sanitary experts, printers, storemen, veterinary surgeons, postal workers, hospital staffs, and prison warders.

The expansion of Britain's army in the space of two years from seven to seventy divisions was an astonishing achievement for a nation that had always resolutely turned its back on militarism. More remarkable still, it was carried out largely without recourse to conscription. By the end of 1914 no fewer than 1,186,337 men had volunteered to serve. Not until January 1916 did Britain need to introduce compulsory enlistment, which both France and Germany had practised for decades.

But the problems raised by this vast expansion were correspondingly huge. The new divisions had to be supplied with uniforms, fed, housed, equipped, and trained. There was accommodation in barracks for only 175,000 single men when war broke out, so most new recruits were found billets in private houses until sufficient huts and tents were available. The country was scoured for clothing firms able to supply material for uniforms: half a sovereign was given to every man willing in the meantime to continue wearing his own suit, boots, and greatcoat. Every single item of equipment was soon in short supply, and factories all over the country were hastily commissioned to meet the demands. Thirty thousand items, all different, were named by the Army in its Official Stores List, ranging from heavy howitzers right down to the humble notice-board drawing-pin, and most of them had now to be produced in hitherto undreamt-of numbers. That quotas were so often reached shows how committed the nation's industries had become to the common cause.

The New Armies were, however, to remain deficient in one respect which no amount of goodwill could remedy: they needed officers, both commissioned and non-commissioned, to train and lead them; but such experienced men were now scarce, and few could be spared from those already at the front.

Kitchener did what he could. Five hundred officers on leave from India were detained and posted to newly-formed units in Britain. Officers and N.C.O.'s from Boer War days were dug out of their retirement and brought back into circulation. Two hundred University candidates, presumably with some relevant qualifications, were given commissions after a token period of training. And twenty thousand 'gentlemen' were commissioned for no good reason whatever except that they were, by the standards of the time, indisputably 'gentlemen'.

The deficiencies were perhaps most glaring at the opposite extremes of the chain of command. The shortage of trained corporals and sergeants meant that the most basic military skills went untaught, or were acquired only by laborious study of training manuals, a process infinitely slower than learning by example. But more important, and unfortunately less likely to improve with time, was the very serious lack of officers with any experience of high command. Of eighteen corps commanders in 1916 (a corps was a formation of three divisions) only two had previously commanded anything as large as a division, and neither of them in time of war. At the Somme on 1 July, of the twenty-three divisional commanders present only three had commanded as much as a brigade before the War. 'Such are the penalties of making do with a small peacetime army' (John Terraine, *The Smoke and the Fire*, Sidgwick and Jackson, 1980).

But there was more at fault than inexperience. The system itself was flawed.

Haldane, the brilliant Liberal War Secretary in the decade before the War, had streamlined the formerly clumsy Army administration, creating the framework for a highly efficient Regular Army Expeditionary Force, and organising the old Militia and Volunteers into a potentially powerful second line of defence, the Territorial Army. To his wide-ranging reforms, often carried through in the teeth of violent opposition from within the Army itself, may be credited much of the success of the B.E.F. in the first weeks of the War. But Haldane had done little to remedy what can now be seen as the British Army's most fundamental defect: the entirely pernicious influence which one class of society – the leisured rich – continued to exercise over the selection of new officers, and over the promotion of existing officers to positions of higher responsibility.

Deeply entrenched in the military mind was the notion that soldiering was an activity best left to gentlemen – a gentleman being defined as someone who did not require to work for his living, and who had been to a good school. (A

'good' school was of course an English Public School; entry
to these, too, was necessarily restricted to the wealthy.) The
sons of shire-county landowners and the offspring of the
lesser nobility were the candidates most likely to meet the
requirements – unexacting and irrelevant to modern warfare
as these were – of the officer selection boards; and in due
course, with the amazing physical courage of their class, they
led their men to futile and needless annihilation on 1 July,
1916, the start of the Battle of the Somme.

But by then there were already signs that the Army,
painfully and with much anguished soul-searching, was
preparing to recognise and accept the facts of modern
warfare; 1 July merely accelerated the pace of change. The
War had developed into – some would say degenerated into –
a battle of rival technologies, in which practical and scientific
talents were just as important as any of the more traditional
military virtues. In the front line, where the appalling new
forces of destruction had daily to be faced, courage counted
as much as ever; but courage alone was no longer enough.
The next generation of officers and N.C.O.'s, who would fill
the gaps left by the battles of Mons, Le Cateau, First and
Second Ypres, Neuve Chapelle, Loos, and 1 July on the
Somme, would need to show greater intelligence, more
adaptability, more resourcefulness, and acquire much more
mechanical and technical expertise, if they were to avoid
repeating the mistakes of their predecessors.

Fortunately there had always existed, unrecognised, just
such a reservoir of talent; and now at last the Army had been
given a chance to tap it. The opportunity was seized, and for
a space of three years, until the War was safely won, place
and privilege were to be reckoned of less account than skill
and enterprise. When the victorious 'Civilian Army' returned
home in 1919 the old bad habits soon re-appeared, as was
perhaps inevitable. But the British Army, to its credit, has
never quite forgotten the lessons of the Great War; nor
should the country as a whole ever forget the part played
during that critical period of its history by those millions of
unconscripted 'amateur soldiers'.

CHAPTER 3

The 51st (Highland) Division

The first unit of the British Expeditionary Force to step on to French soil after the outbreak of war, a battalion of the Argyll & Sutherland Highlanders, disembarked unobtrusively at Boulogne towards the end of the first week; its immediate duty was to organise the defence of the lines of communication of the main contingent that would follow.

At Mons, and in the great Retreat, every Scottish regiment of the Regular Army was represented by at least one of its battalions. The 2nd Dragoons (Royal Scots Greys) formed part of the Cavalry Division, but all the others were infantrymen: 1st Scots Guards, 2nd Royal Scots, 1st and 2nd Royal Scots Fusiliers, 2nd King's Own Scottish Borderers, 1st Cameronians, 2nd Highland Light Infantry, 2nd Seaforth Highlanders, 1st Gordon Highlanders, 1st Cameron Highlanders, 1st Black Watch, and the 2nd Argyll & Sutherland Highlanders. How these highly professional Regular soldiers acquitted themselves in the first months of War has already been described. They fought with unwavering skill and gallantry, but their losses in dead and wounded, against such a powerful and well-prepared foe, soon reached alarming proportions.

For instance, the 2nd Cameronians – their Regimental name commemorated the martyred Covenanter Richard Cameron, and it was said of Cameronians that they 'made every battle a new exercise of their faith' – came out of the battle of Neuve Chapelle (March 1915) with 150 men and just one officer, a subaltern.

Even as early as September 1914 it was becoming evident that Kitchener's assumptions regarding the length and magnitude of the conflict were not unreasonable, and that the Army would have to dig deeply into the nation's resources of manpower before the struggle was over.

Men of the Black Watch resting near Contalmaison, on the Somme, in October, 1916. In the middle distance are crosses on newly-dug graves. The ground, though soft, is not yet the quagmire which it became towards the end of that autumn.

The Regular Army maintained Reserves of trained, time-expired men who could be called upon to provide rapid reinforcement of depleted battalions. In addition, each Regular battalion possessed one or more Territorial battalions bearing its Regimental name; and these battalions of partly-trained, 'week-end' soldiers were a ready source of additional manpower. By law no Territorial soldier was obliged to serve outside the United Kingdom: indeed, the defence of the homeland was the Territorial Army's *raison d'être*. But in fact nearly all Territorials were more than willing to waive this privilege, and almost to a man they signed the 'General Service Obligation', giving the Army the right to send them wherever it wished.

It had been laid down that at least six months' training should be given to every Territorial Battalion after mobilisation, but such niceties were ignored in this time of crisis, and the war had been in progress less than six weeks when the first Territorial battalion, the London Scottish, landed in France to join the Regular divisions. At Messines on 31 October they went into action for the first time, sustaining 394 casualties.

Twenty-two Territorial battalions were fighting in France by the end of 1914, and no fewer than eleven Territorial *divisions*, each consisting of twelve infantry battalions, plus their own divisional artillery and ancillary services, were actively engaged on the Western Front by November 1916, when the Battle of Beaumont Hamel was fought.

One of these, the 51st (Highland) Division, whose attack on Beaumont Hamel is described in this book, began the War with all the disadvantages inevitably experienced by second-line forces who have to rely on short-sighted and niggardly employers. Over the past seventy years much has been written concerning the 'incompetence' of British military commanders in the War, almost all such criticism being based on their apparent indifference to mounting casualties during the various lengthy Allied offensives. Not enough has been said of the gross failure of those guardians of the public purse, the politicians, to provide the Army commanders with the men and the means that might have made these offensives more rapidly successful.

The 51st Division, on its arrival in mid-August 1914 at its war station outside Bedford, a pleasant county town fifty miles north of London, found itself obliged to make do with the most ancient equipment, absurdly inadequate training facilities (no rifle ranges, scarcely any practice ammunition), obsolete transport, and an almost complete absence of staff.

What the newly-formed Division did *not* lack was enthusiasm, and that commodity, along with an unusual ability to improvise, compensated to a large extent for material deficiencies. Morale among the men was sky-high in those first weeks, partly reflecting the euphoria which the country as a whole was experiencing, but not least because of the friendly welcome they had received from the local inhabitants.

The sudden appearance in their midst of 18,000 young

men, with their unintelligible accents, outlandish dress, and bizarre foreign customs, merely provoked in the tolerant citizens of Bedford a reaction of genuine interest, coupled with a warm concern for the invaders' welfare. Highland reels were soon, to the skirl of the Regimental bagpipes, being danced in Bedford market square; Highland Games were organised in the local parks; and on New Year's Eve local civic dignitaries joined the Highlanders in their annual tribal feasting. To everyone's astonishment – not least, perhaps, to the astonishment of understandably apprehensive Staff officers – crime rates were subsequently found to have *dropped* in the Bedford area with the arrival of the 'rude, licentious soldiery': responding to the kindness shown to them by the townspeople, the visitors were clearly determined to be on their very best behaviour.

Sadly, the removal of so many youngsters from isolated country areas to a densely-populated urban setting also exposed them to one curious, though predictable, hazard. During the first winter in Bedford 529 cases of measles were diagnosed by the divisional Medical Officers. Inoculation against the disease was not available at that time, and antibiotics had yet to be discovered. More than fifty deaths resulted before the epidemic waned. These Highland lads must have possessed little natural resistance to what was, for them, a dangerous foreign scourge.

Not all the units which made up the Highland Division were from rural communities, however, though it probably included more deerstalkers, gillies, and gamekeepers – and no doubt more poachers – than any other division in the Army. Such men needed comparatively little training to become superb snipers and scouts. Many men, too, had in civilian life been shepherds, farmhands, or forestry workers, and so were used to long hours of arduous work in the open air. These found it easy to cope with the physical demands imposed by strenuous military training. Very few Highland Division territorials were ill-formed, stunted, malnourished products of industrial city slums, such as were to shock the conscience of the nation when they first came to light in the ranks of Kitchener's 'New Armies'. But relative poverty and deprivation still lurked in some parts of the Highlands, and many men would have had to admit that living conditions at Bedford Camp were a distinct improvement on what they had known at home.

Training, despite manifold difficulties of administration and a continuing lack of basic equipment, proceeded apace, and in May of 1915 the Division moved to France to await the summons to battle. Bedford Camp remained as one of several training depots which the Division used to feed its ranks following battle losses. At first, only two of its brigades were composed of battalions from Scottish Highland regiments: the third brigade, in the temporary absence of sufficient numbers of trained Highland troops, had been cobbled together from four battalions recruited in Lancashire! Such, however, had been the response in Scotland to Kitchener's appeal that, with 500,000 Scottish recruits to choose from, there were soon more than enough trained Scots available to maintain the strength of all twelve of the Highland Division's battalions, as well as to fill three 'New Army' Scottish divisions – the 9th, the 15th, and the 52nd (Lowland) Division.

The 51st Division recruited mainly north of the Highland Line – that is, from the counties of Caithness, Sutherland, Ross and Cromarty, Inverness-shire, the Inner and Outer Hebrides, Argyllshire, Nairn, Moray, Banff, Aberdeenshire, Perthshire, Angus, and Kincardine: a very large area, but one with a small total population. The constituent battalions usually had clearly-defined catchment areas: for example, the 6th Seaforths recruited only in Morayshire, the 4th Gordons only in the city of Aberdeen, and the 5th Gordons only in the bleak, sparsely-populated region of Buchan.

The advantages of this system were obvious: men could join up confident of finding in their local unit a few old friends, possibly some relatives, and certainly many acquaintances.

The disadvantage, not apparent until later, was that a tightly-knit community could suddenly find itself mourning the loss of most of its menfolk in just one costly battle. Many such communities were in the industrial north of England; in Scotland the ill effects of local recruiting were less dramatic, but in the long run equally devastating. Turriff, a small, agricultural township on the Aberdeenshire-Banff border, found itself at the conclusion of the War with scarcely enough young men left alive to continue the working of its once-thriving farms. On the Somme, at Arras, at Passchendaele, at Cambrai, and in the German and British offensives of 1918 the Highland Division was generally in the thick of the fighting; and Turriff, which had recruited almost exclusively into battalions used by the Highland Division, earned for itself the dubious distinction of having lost more of its menfolk than any other place in Britain.

That might be hard to prove; but statistics for another Highland Division recruiting area, the Isle of Lewis in the Outer Hebrides, show that from a total population of 29,603 no fewer than 6712 men enlisted, of whom 1151 died (T.C. Smout, *A Century of the Scottish People*, Collins, 1980). According to one reliable authority (D. Duff, *Scotland's War Losses*, Glasgow, 1947), Scotland as a whole, with a total of 110,000 war dead, had the highest mortality relative to its population of any part of the Empire; and certainly no Scottish region was harder hit than the Highlands.

When the war ended, the losses of the 51st Division had reached a total of 5668 dead and 7717 'missing'; most of the latter are now known definitely to have been killed. In addition, at least 30,000 men of the Division were wounded, many being permanently disabled in body or mind. Foch, the Commander-in-Chief of all the Allied Armies at the end of the War, spoke of the Highland Division as being 'among the most valorous and the most sternly tried of all the troops on the Western Front'.

For the northern counties of Scotland the price of victory was almost too high. Not only were casualties among men

Grim-looking Gordon Highlanders, about to take over newly-captured trenches, are passed by ammunition limbers on the Albert-Bapaume Road near La Boisselle, July 1916.

recruited there as great as in any part of the kingdom, but, as in all regions which supported a popular Territorial unit, the calibre of the men who died had been particularly high. These were individuals who in times of peace would, through their various professions, have led the nation: not by reason of inherited wealth or privilege, for their origins were sometimes extremely humble, but by their own native ability, their gifts of imagination and intellect, and the compelling force of their personalities.

Something of this can be glimpsed in those solemn *Books of Remembrance* which schools and universities compiled with loving care in the post-War years. There one may read brief biographical details of the alumni who perished, and the waste of bright talent is all too evident. Twelve of Aberdeen University's former students fell during the assault on Beaumont Hamel in November 1916: each of their short life-histories reveals a 'promise of greatness' which, while it goes far to explain the unsurpassed reputation of the Highland Division in battle, can only make us more keenly aware of all the peacetime skills which were irrevocably lost to Scotland in the muddy trenches of the Western Front.

Here, chosen more or less at random, are two of those entries:

> Rev. Norman Crichton: 2nd Lieutenant, 4th Battalion Seaforth Highlanders; son of William Crichton, mason, Stornoway; born there, 3 February 1888; graduated M.A., 1911; student for three years at Aberdeen U.F. College.
>
> In October 1914 he enlisted as a Private in the 4th Gordon Highlanders, and was afterwards commissioned as 2nd Lieutenant in the 4th Seaforths. Before proceeding abroad he was licensed as a probationer by the U.F. Presbytery of Lewis. He rendered distinguished service as a bombing officer in France, and fell in action at Beaumont Hamel on 15 November 1916. Celtic fervour and eloquence, combined with a thorough scholarship, marked Crichton as one who would have proved a highly successful minister. His name is recorded on the Thiepval Memorial.
>
> Robert William Ferguson: 2nd Lieutenant, 5th Battalion Gordon Highlanders; son of Alexander Ferguson, painter; born at Peterhead, 20 October, 1887; educated at Peterhead Academy; entered Aberdeen University 1905; graduated M.A. with honours in Mathematics, 1909; B.Sc., 1910. He was a keen student of nature, took a special course of Botany at Oxford University, and had gathered much valuable material concerning the Flora of Banffshire with a view to publication. He proved himself a very successful teacher, doing work at Aberlour, Nairn and Sharpe's Institute, Perth; he took up the Boy Scout movement with great enthusiasm and was popular with both parents and pupils.
>
> In April 1915 he enlisted in his old College Company, the 4th Gordon Highlanders, was later commissioned in the 5th Battalion and thereafter was appointed Musketry Officer. Ferguson went through his training at Aberdeen, Peterhead and Ripon and crossed to France in 1916, took part in the early Somme Battles and was killed in action at Beaumont Hamel, 13 November 1916. He is buried at Hawthorn Ridge Cemetry, No. 2, Auchonvillers, Row B, Grave 60.

CHAPTER 4

Trenches and Wire

At six o'clock one Spring evening in 1918, near St Quentin, a young gunnery officer, the son of a Scottish farmer, was suddenly informed that a communication trench five feet deep and at least 150 feet long had to be dug behind his guns before midnight. It was, he recalled, a tall order. The men were already weary after a strenuous day. He told them to rest for an hour and get something to eat. Meanwhile, he himself set to work:

> It was an exceptionally warm evening for March. I cast off my tunic and my shirt, took the shovel and made a start on the trench behind one of the guns. I worked hard. By the end of the hour I had made a trench over three yards long which was five feet deep, three feet wide at the bottom and four feet wide at the top. The sergeants couldn't believe their eyes when they returned from the cookhouse and saw what I had done. Now there wasn't the slightest suggestion that the task was impossible . . .

That trench, which his men successfully completed on time, not only saved Lieutenant Carr's own life when the Germans attacked the next day, 21 March, but it also enabled his battery to function effectively throughout the heaviest enemy barrage of the War. (The incident is one of many experiences vividly recalled in Carr's fascinating memoir, *A Time to leave the Ploughshares*, Hale, 1985).

'Sweat saves blood' was a maxim familiar to every old soldier; 'dig or die' expressed the same theme even more succinctly in World War 2. In the earlier conflict a vast amount of labour was expended on the construction of defensive trench systems, which became more and more elaborate as time went on. Previous wars – the American Civil War of 1861-65 and the Russo-Japanese War of 1904-05

31

A sentry on the firestep of a trench near Arras, January 1918. The sides of this deep, well-constructed trench are protected against erosion with wire-netting and metal pickets. Part of the trench has been roofed over to provide some shelter from the elements.

in particular – had shown that a direct assault on a strongly entrenched position would almost always fail, yet both armies, and especially the British, made such an attempt repeatedly from 1915 onwards. Neither side had done much training in peacetime either in the construction or in the tactics of entrenchment, but the Germans had enough theoretical knowledge to give them a significant early advantage.

A typical trench system of 1916, such as was present in the Somme sector, consisted of three or four roughly parallel lines of trenches, separated from each other by distances of from 100 to 400 yards. The front line might typically be held by two companies, the middle line (or lines) by a third company, and the last or reserve line by a fourth company along with the Battalion Headquarters. The total length of front held by one battalion varied considerably, from as much as 1000 yards in a quiet sector to as little as a couple of hundred in one with a bad reputation. In a particularly active

Entrance stair to a German dug-out captured by the 9th (Scottish) Division on 3 July, 1916. Many German dug-outs had two stories and were well furnished, some even possessing electric light, comfortable chairs, and pictures on the walls. More significantly, they were deep enough to withstand the heaviest artillery bombardment.

sector another complete trench system might be constructed behind the first, and sometimes even a third system behind that.

No trench ran straight for more than a few yards, thus minimising the damage that an enemy raider could inflict firing along its length. Forward-facing 'fire-bays' alternated with solid earth 'traverses' to give the trench, as seen from the air, its distinctive 'square-wave' appearance.

German barbed wire at Beaumont Hamel after the attack in November, 1916. Despite intensive shelling, enough wire remains to form a severe hazard to infantry advancing without cover from tanks.

Linking all these lines was an irregular network of minor communication trenches, designed to allow rapid switching of troops forwards, backwards, or to adjacent sectors, as circumstances demanded. After dark, especially, the main approach trench, which usually ran back to a concealed entry in a relatively safe area, become the focus of intense activity. Along it, on their way up to the front, trudged endless relays of men laden with supplies: boxes of small-arms ammunition, Mills bombs, rifle grenades, and shells for Stokes mortars; coils of barbed wire for fresh entanglements; heavy timbers for trench maintenance and the reinforcement of dug-outs; food and water rations; cooking fuel, toilet articles, mailbags – all the thousand and one items needed to ensure the efficiency of the battalion in the field. Not surprisingly, approach trenches came in for special attention from the opposing artillery. Regular shelling, and the heavy wear and tear of their nightly human traffic, often reduced them to mere mud-filled channels. Some German approach trenches

By 1918 German wire entanglements were hundreds of yards in depth. This was the obstacle facing the Australians in 1918 in front of the Beaurevoir line.

were skilfully camouflaged with canvas roof-screens, or covered with hurdles and netting, to conceal them from aerial observers.

Like the approach and communication trenches, the fire trenches were constructed to give protection against shell splinters and shrapnel; but in addition they were designed to enable the defenders to detect and repel enemy assaults. A typical fire trench in 1916 was some six to twelve feet wide at the top, tapering to about three feet wide at the bottom. The closer the walls of the trench, the greater the protection against shell splinters, but a narrow trench was more readily blocked by debris. The best compromise was to vary the width, and during a bombardment the occupants sought shelter in the narrower segments, where the risks from flying metal were less.

The earth which had been dug out from the trench was heaped up in front to form the parapet and behind to form the parados. Where the water-table lay close to the surface,

German barbed wire, of unorthodox design, near Arras in 1917. Trench mortars and field artillery were better than heavy guns for breaching such entanglements. Tanks were effective at flattening wire, but were apt to become bogged down in the mud, or get stuck in a shell-hole, while crossing No-Man's-Land.

as in many parts of Flanders, the trench might have to be no more than three feet deep, in which case both parapet and parados were formed of layers of sandbags supported with wire-netting. To stop bullets effectively, the parapet had to be at least five feet wide. Skilfully camouflaged loopholes, sometimes shielded with thick steel plating, enabled snipers to keep the trenches opposite under constant surveillance. After the battle of Neuve Chapelle (March 1915) the Germans built machine-gun emplacements into their parapets at intervals of twenty yards or so. These consisted of large V-shaped wooden boxes, the apex of the V pointing towards the enemy and reinforced with a steel loophole, the whole box being well sandbagged. From within the box, firing at near ground-level, the machine-gunner had a wide field of fire, yet remained almost invisible to his opponents.

Several days might pass without a glimpse of the enemy, but in the event of an enemy attack across No-Man's-Land the alarm would be sounded by the sentries, and the fire-step – a raised platform on the forward face of the trench – would be immediately manned by every available rifleman and Lewis-gunner.

'Saps' were trenches dug surreptitiously towards the enemy lines for purposes of eavesdropping and gathering military intelligence, or to provide forward starting-points for trench raiding parties. One type, called a 'Russian' sap, was dug as a tunnel with only a few feet of earth above it. When a small explosive charge was detonated, the roof of the tunnel collapsed, so that a shallow trench was formed, down which assaulting troops could pass rapidly and safely. Russian saps were employed to good effect in the attack on Beaumont Hamel in November 1916.

By joining up several saps a new front-line trench could be created ahead of the old one. Such work was naturally fraught with hazard, even when carried out under cover of darkness, but experience had shown that no advance across No-Man's-Land was likely to succeed if the width to be crossed was more than 250 yards. On 1 July the infantry in many places had to cover twice that distance. On the other hand, if the opposing trenches were too close, then a barrage dropping on the enemy's front line would be liable to cause casualties among the attackers.

Trenches required constant maintenance to remain usable. Sandbags, wire netting, hurdles of brushwood, pit props, and old railway sleepers were the materials employed to shore up the sides of the trench against erosion by the elements. In very wet weather – the autumn of 1916 was notorious for its rainfall – even the best constructed trench gradually filled up with liquid mud, rendering useless the slatted wooden duck-boards laid along the floor. As early as 1915 the Germans kept some of their trenches dry by means of mechanical pumps working continuously.

Before the great assault on 1 July, 1916, General Rawlinson advised his corps commanders that nothing could survive the British preliminary bombardment, and the

Teutonic thoroughness in defence. One of the vast barbed-wire entanglements encountered by the Canadians in front of the Hindenburg Line during the Allies' advance in the final weeks of the War.

infantry would only have to walk across and take possession of the German trenches. But the enemy, given clear and ample warning of the impending attack, had spent the time constructing a warren of excellent dug-outs, some large enough to accommodate whole battalions, and deep enough to withstand the heaviest shells. Hewn out of the Somme chalk to a depth of more than twenty-five feet, these shelters were provided with several entrances, gas-proof doors, and even mechanical air-filters. When the British barrage lifted, their occupants emerged almost unscathed and proceeded to wreak havoc with rifle and machine-gun on the slowly advancing lines of infantry.

British trenches were seldom as elaborate or comfortable as these German ones, since it was never the British intention to remain on the defensive for long. German trenches and dug-outs captured on the Somme were something of a revelation, and thereafter the best British trenches could stand comparison with those of the enemy, in efficiency if not elegance.

On 15 September, 1914, when the B.E.F. was first given the order to entrench, the day was spent, according to the *Official History*, 'improving the trenches and collecting wire from the fences of the country round, which was converted at night into entanglements; for except what the Field Companies carried, no barbed wire or other engineer stores were yet available'. In this respect the Germans were again at an advantage, for the previous day a whole trainload of stores for siege warfare had reached them. All through that first autumn the British suffered from a lack of barbed wire, and at times were reduced to making do with coils of plain, unbarbed fence-wire 'borrowed' from neighbouring farms.

The use of barbed wire increased enormously as the War settled down into mutual siege operations. At first the entanglements, set up some yards beyond the front-line trenches, consisted of no more than a few strands of barbed wire, strung from metal pickets. By 1915 the Germans often dug a ditch in front of their parapet which they filled with coils of wire invisible from the British lines. By 1918, especially on the German side of No-Man's-Land, entanglements were hundreds of yards in depth and impenetrable except by tanks. German barbed wire – said to be 'as thick as a man's thumb' – was particularly difficult to cut by shellfire. Many attacks failed on 1 July, 1916, when the attackers came up against almost intact wire. Even at Beaumont Hamel in November of that same year, after every effort had been made to solve the problem, lives were still lost as men groped in vain for gaps in dense entanglements.

Where trenches were close, paths could be blown in the wire by using 'Bangalore torpedoes' – lengths of 2-inch sheet-iron cylinders packed with gun-cotton. Pushed surreptitiously under the enemy wire and fired, these cleared a lane wide enough for a raiding party; but for larger operations shelling was to remain the only solution other than the use of tanks.

The simple combination of trench and barbed wire, crude as it seems, brought to a standstill for nearly four years the world's most powerful armies. In the end it was not so much a crumbling of the German defence system as a disintegration of German morale which brought the War to its conclusion.

CHAPTER 5

Tunnels and Mines

Before the advent of reliable tanks, fortifications which could neither be battered into submission by gunfire, nor captured by direct infantry assault, might yet be made to yield to a very old form of siegecraft: mining.

Besieging armies had used tunnels to undermine fortress walls and to breach defences long before gunpowder changed the face of war; but with the invention of explosives military tunnelling assumed increased importance. On the Western Front some 25,000 men were employed solely on tunnel work. Many of them had been miners before joining up. Their courage, in conditions most men would find beyond endurance, was to become legendary.

The biggest and best-known mining operation of the War was carried out in 1917 on Messines Ridge, south of Ypres, where at 3.10 a.m. on 7 June nineteen mines containing a million pounds of explosives were detonated simultaneously under the German lines. But the previous year, 1916, had in fact witnessed the peak of mining activity. In the course of it the British blew no fewer than 750 mines, and their opponents 696. Corresponding totals for 1917 were 117 and 106.

In constructing a mine, a vertical shaft was first sunk from a position in or near the front line. The excavated material, especially in chalky regions like the Somme, had to be disposed of at a distance if the new working was not to be detected from the air. When the shaft had been sunk to the required depth – for example, a shaft 125 feet deep was dug at St Eloi on the Messines Ridge – the horizontal portion was begun. This might take the form of a single direct tunnel driven straight forwards to the enemy position, but more often a number of side galleries were also excavated, at an

A rare photograph of miners at work. It shows an explosive charge being laid in a tunnel during the battle of the Somme. Note the white Somme chalk. The officer on the left is using the acoustic device called a Geophone to detect sounds of enemy counter-mining.

angle to the main tunnel, so that a herringbone pattern resulted. These side galleries were used as listening posts; from them, with a simple acoustic rangefinder called a Geophone, a trained listener could plot, up to a distance of several hundred feet and with precise directional accuracy, the approach of enemy counter-tunnellers.

Thus there developed below ground, chiefly in the zone of the First Army north of Arras, but also on the Somme and south of Ypres, a type of warfare just as grim and bloody, and without question as nerve-racking to its participants, as that which raged on the surface many feet above them. It was fought for the most part in silence. Insulated from the crump of exploding shells and the stutter of machine-guns, the tunneller inched his way forward by prising pieces of rock loose with a grafting tool – a bayonet fitted with a handle worked well – passing the debris back at intervals for conveyance to the surface. He used his pick sparingly, for the sound it made carried great distances through the layers of rock, and could alert the enemy. Mostly he worked naked, lying on his side in a cavity less than three feet by five feet; anything larger was considered a waste of labour.

All the normal hazards of mining had to be faced – sudden falls of rock, inundation by underground springs, the presence of deadly invisible mine-gas and carbon monoxide. But to these was added a new peril: the risk of a lonely and agonising death from enemy action.

As each miner knew, no sooner was a fresh shaft begun than counter-measures were put in hand by the other side. Into a gallery dug rapidly to intercept the new tunnel would be placed a charge just large enough to destroy both the tunnel and its occupants. Such undercharged mines were called 'camouflets', and they had the advantage of not cratering the surface. In June, 1916, near Petit Bois south of Ypres, a camouflet laid by the Germans destroyed 150 feet of a tunnel being dug by a party of twelve British miners. Eleven of the miners died, but the twelfth succeeded in finding a pocket of air was eventually dug out alive by a rescue team after being entombed for no less than six days.

Occasionally, either by accident or design, an enemy gallery might be broken into. A desperate fight with picks and knives could result; but if the gallery was found unoccupied, a charge would be left hidden in it and exploded when the enemy was heard returning.

Australian troops provided many of the best miners on the Western Front. They brought with them from Australia their 'Wombat', a hand-operated boring machine that could drill a 200-foot-long hole, 6½ inches in diameter, at a rate of three or four feet per hour in chalk, or four to six feet per hour in clay. Four men could work on the machine at a time. On one occasion, sound-detectors revealed that the enemy was in the act of charging a nearby mine. 'Wombat' was immediately brought into action, and the Australians bored rapidly through ninety-seven feet of hard chalk and flint to where the mine lay. A cartridge was then inserted along the bore-hole, and both mine and tunnel were successfully destroyed.

During the great mining operation at Messines Ridge in 1917 a German counter-mining gallery was found to have approached within eighteen inches of a vital British mine beneath Hill 60. The temptation to blow the mine prematurely was great, but General Plumer wisely refused his permission, and the enemy tunnellers luckily came no closer. Of the twenty mines laid on that occasion, only one was discovered and blown by the enemy before the battle began.

As skills in sound-location increased, the ability to excavate rapidly became paramount. New tunnels had to be dug, explosives – weighing many tons, in some instances – laid in place at the tunnel head, and all the necessary electrical connections made, before the opposition could organise effective counter-measures. A rate of fifteen feet in twenty-four hours was considered average, but double that might be achieved in clay. The record in chalk was a prodigious sixty-two feet in one day, and there the tunnel was large enough in cross-section to allow infantry to pass, as well as being fully timbered for extra strength.

Sometimes, when the enemy was known to be close and possibly already suspicious, the rate of progress might have to be kept down to as little as a couple of feet in twenty-four hours. This was so at La Boisselle, on the Albert-Bapaume road, before the opening of the 1916 July offensive. There two huge mines, 'Lochnagar' and 'Y Sap', were to be fired at two minutes before Zero. Even as the charges were being stealthily placed in position the tunnellers could clearly overhear the Germans counter-tunnelling nearby.

'Lochnagar', the largest mine ever exploded on the Western Front, left a crater – still visible today – some three hundred feet wide, ninety feet deep, with a lip fifteen feet high. It destroyed nine dug-outs packed with Germans, but did little to assist the attacking infantry, mostly Tyneside Scottish and Tyneside Irish, who were all but wiped out by the inevitable German machine-guns using cross-fire from intact positions.

Hawthorn mine exploding on 1 July 1916. Most of one German company were entombed, but the crater was back in German hands within a matter of hours. A further mine was laid by the British in the same place in November 1916 and fired at Zero Hour on 13 November.

The explosive most often used in such mines was ammonal, a mixture of ammonium nitrate, powdered aluminium, and charcoal; comparatively safe to handle, but detonating with shattering effect. Once the charge had been placed in position – twenty-seven tons of it at 'Lochnagar' – the mine chamber was sealed off from the outlet of the tunnel with many sandbags, so that the force of the explosion was exerted chiefly upwards through the ground, where it could do most damage.

Caught on film in one of the War's most dramatic images, the firing of the Hawthorn Redoubt mine at Zero minus ten minutes on 1 July, 1916, was graphically described by a German officer:

> During the intense bombardment there was a terrific explosion which for the moment completely drowned the thunder of the artillery. A great cloud of smoke rose up from the trenches of No. 9 Company, followed by a tremendous shower of stones, which seemed to fall from the sky all over our position. More than three sections of No. 9 Company were blown into the air, and the neighbouring dug-outs were broken in and blocked. The ground all round was white with the debris of chalk as if it had been snowing, and a gigantic

crater, over fifty yards in diameter and some sixty feet deep gaped like an open wound in the side of the hill.

Ten minutes were allowed by the British Corps Commander for debris from the Hawthorn mine explosion to settle before the infantry advanced: an error that would cost his men dear. The expert Inspector of Mines had correctly recommended firing the mine at Zero exactly, since there was plenty of evidence that all sizeable debris from such explosions settled within twenty seconds. He was overruled. The consequences of that ten minutes' delay, in which those of the defenders who had survived the explosion were able to climb from their dug-outs and man their weapons, are discussed in Chapter 12.

Four and a half months later, the 51st Division was ordered to attack the same sector. A fresh mine was dug beneath Hawthorn Crater, and on this occasion it was exploded at Zero precisely, with spectacularly successful results.

The operation on Messines Ridge in June 1917 proved to be the last great mining enterprise of the War. Thereafter the tank became the principal means employed by the British for breaking into the enemy's defences, superseding both the use of mines and prolonged artillery bombardments. Lacking tanks in significant numbers, the Germans had to rely on heavy artillery in the initial stages of their 1918 offensives. They had more or less abandoned mining after the Messines Ridge battle, though why they did so remains a matter for speculation. Probably they decided that offensive mining was too costly in men and materials that could both be better employed elsewhere, and too uncertain in its results against an alert and determined enemy.

CHAPTER 6

Rifles, Machine-Guns, Grenades

The B.E.F.'s reputation in 1914 rested on the almost legendary skill of its infantry in musketry. In a battalion there were as many as 1000 riflemen – for at that time specialisation was less common – and every man had been trained to a high level of competence. In the so-called 'mad minute' of rapid fire a rate of fifteen rounds per minute was attainable by most of the men, and many units possessed experts who could approach double that rate.

This represented a formidable weight of firepower against enemy infantry advancing across open ground, especially when delivered, as it often was, from well-chosen concealed positions. Moreover it was 'aimed' fire, where every bullet was likely to find its mark, as witness the heaps of German dead left at every stage of their advance to the Marne. Even at First Ypres the British were still relying far more on rifles than on machine-guns; only two Maxim guns had been issued to each battalion, and many of these were by that time damaged and unusable.

The Short Magazine Lee Enfield rifle, Mark 1, which the Army had adopted as its standard weapon after the Boer War, was the end-result of various design improvements made over the previous half-century. By 1914 the rifle, like some successful animal species, had arrived at a state beyond which it hardly needed to evolve further. It passed with distinction the severest tests of war. At 8lb 10½oz (4 kg) it was light enough to be carried long distances, yet its bolt mechanism, which was exceptionally rapid in action, was sufficiently robust to withstand rough handling. The detachable box magazine held 10 rounds of .303 ammunition; riflemen normally carried 120 rounds each in pouches, with an extra 50 or 100 rounds in bandoliers during an attack. The

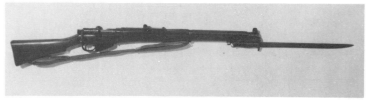

Short Magazine Lee Enfield rifle, Mark 3. Shown here with its 18-inch bayonet attached, this was the standard British weapon issued in 1916. In expert hands it could kill at a range of two-thirds of a mile. At least fifteen rounds a minute could be fired by most Regular riflemen in 1914.

rifle's foresight was a vertical blade, its nearsight a U-notch; earlier models were fitted with long-range sights, for the weapon in skilled hands could be effective at 3000 yards or more. At 500 yards it was lethal. In the trenches its worst enemy was mud, though it was less susceptible to stoppages from that cause than were machine-guns.

The Army School of Musketry at Hythe had thoroughly absorbed the lesson of the Boer War, where the rebel guerillas had managed to inflict alarming casualties with their skilful shooting. It was that experience, together with the rejection on grounds of expense of a request by the School in 1909 that the number of machine-guns be increased from two to four per battalion, which had led to more intensive rifle-training. With the vast expansion of the Army from 1914 onwards, a steady decline in the standard of musketry was inevitable. There were insufficient instructors to go round, and not nearly enough practice ammunition. By 1916, standards had declined so drastically that few men could now hit enemy targets at 300 yards, whereas before the War accurate shooting up to thrice that distance has been commonplace. Describing one incident in July 1916 the Official Historian writes:

> Far more execution could have been done had the infantry made better musketry practice on the retiring enemy . . . (so) in despair, officers took up rifles and picked off fleeing Germans until the machine-guns could be brought forward.

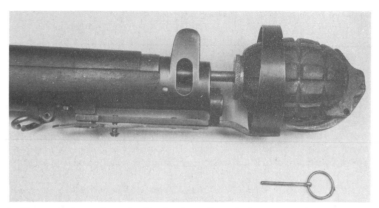

A rifle grenade ready to be fired. The safety pin has been withdrawn, but the firing lever is held securely in a ring attached to the muzzle of the rifle. The grenade is projected from the muzzle by the force of the explosion of a blank cartridge.

Such occasions were admittedly rare during the years of static warfare. In the trenches musketry skills were likely to atrophy from sheer lack of opportunity to exercise them, although individual marksmen were always in demand as snipers: such men were supplied with steel loopholes, more accurate or even telescopic sights, and sometimes with express rifles.

By 1916 the infantryman's main personal weapons were the bayonet and the bomb. The bayonet, a steel blade sixteen inches long which clipped on to the muzzle of the rifle, was a crude but effective instrument in close-quarter fighting. It had particular value where silence was desirable, as in a night raid on an enemy post. Memorable lectures on 'The Spirit of the Bayonet', in which its use was invested with an almost mystical significance, were delivered to horrified audiences of young officers by the fire-eating Colonel Ronald Campbell.

Bombs – grenades as they would now be called – were used in enormous numbers. Every rifleman went into an attack with at least two, while specialists in the bombing platoons were each supplied with twenty or more. In operations of any magnitude, support parties laden with additional supplies followed the assault companies, drawing on huge reserve

Canadian troops of the 8th Winnipeg Battalion receiving bombing instruction, June 1916. Skill in musketry diminished as reliance on grenades increased. For clearing enemy trenches the grenade was often the most effective weapon. 23,000 were carried into the front line for the 51st Division's attack on Beaumont Hamel.

dumps containing, in the case of a two-battalion attack, not fewer than 15,000 grenades. In 1916, 250,000 Mills bombs were manufactured *weekly* at the start of the year, 800,000 per week by July, and by December the output reached the colossal figure of 1,400,000 weekly.

Two main types of grenade were available by 1916: the Mills bomb Number 36, which was designed to be thrown by hand, and the rifle grenade, a bomb so modified that it could be fired a short distance by the standard rifle, with a blank cartridge in place of the usual bullet.

The hand-thrown version weighed twenty-two ounces (625 g.) and contained three ounces (85 g.) of either amatol or ammonal. Shaped something like a pineapple, it had a faceted iron casing which fragmented when the charge inside exploded. The grenade was triggered by a five-second time-fuse set off by releasing a lever. Normally the lever was held securely in place by a pin, but once the pin was withdrawn

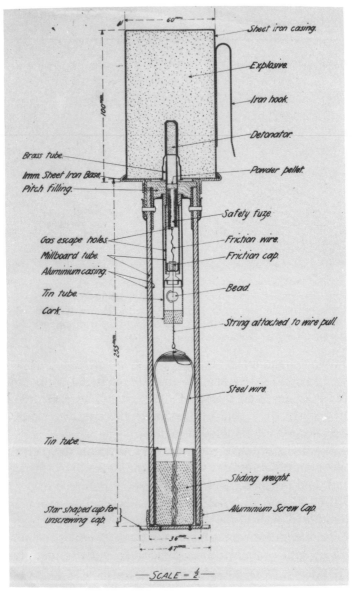

Diagram of German 'potato masher' grenade. The long handle perhaps provided extra leverage, but the British preferred the Mills bomb.

Vickers machine-gunners, wearing gas-helmets, in action on the Somme, July 1916. Each gun had a crew of six. Machine-guns were the supreme weapons of defence in trench warfare, but they were too heavy to be used in close support of an infantry attack.

the lever had to be held down by pressure from the thrower's forefinger. After the bomb left his hand the lever flew off, the fuse mechanism began to operate, and five seconds later the bomb exploded. A cup-shaped device performed for the rifle-grenade the same function as the thrower's hand in preventing the fuse lever from being released prematurely. A rifle grenade could be projected farther than a hand grenade, but with less flexibility of range.

Manufacturing defects caused many bombs used in the initial phases of the Somme fighting to explode prematurely or not at all, but once these troubles were corrected bombing became the method of choice for clearing craters, dug-outs, and trenches. Bombing sections were enlarged to become bombing platoons; sometimes specialist battalion bombing platoons were formed. Almost too great a reliance on the effects of bombs developed, and at the end of the Battle of the Somme a warning was issued against the assumption that one bomb was enough to clear a dug-out; in fact, half a dozen or more might be needed. Particularly effective for such a task was the 'P' grenade, which on bursting produced a dense cloud of asphyxiating white smoke.

To clear an enemy trench, bombers and bayonet men had to work in close cooperation. The bomber hurled his grenade over the traverse into the next bay; when it exploded, the bayonet men dashed forward to finish off survivors and prevent retaliation. This grim procedure was then repeated all along the trench.

The Germans favoured a long-handled grenade shaped like a wooden potato masher. The handle was thought to provide extra leverage, but the evidence is that by 1916 British bombing techniques had gained an ascendancy that was not subsequently lost.

The grenade had a pedigree stretching back at least two centuries. The first wholly automatic machine-gun, in contrast, was only twenty-five years old in 1914, although hand-cranked or motor-driven rapid-firing weapons, of which the Gatling is a good example, had been in use during the American Civil War (1861-65). The Maxim gun of 1889 differed from these in that it relied on the energy of the recoil to eject the spent cartridge and to feed, load, and fire the next round automatically, repeating this sequence for as long as the trigger remained pressed, or until the ammunition belt was emptied.

The Maxim (manufactured as the Vickers in Britain) was adopted by both sides as their standard 'heavy' machine-gun. Each ammunition belt held 250 rounds of .311 calibre, and the rate of fire was 600-700 rounds per minute; short bursts of fire conserved ammunition. A solidly-built tripod stand, weighing some 20 pounds (9 kg.) ensured stability during firing. The gun itself weighed 38½ pounds (17 kg.) including the water in the cooling-jacket round the barrel. Two men carried the gun and the tripod, another two the ammunition belts, and each machine-gun detachment had two men as replacements. Its weight made the gun unsuitable for close support in an attack, but in defence, its principal rôle, it

A Lewis gunner, at his post near Wancourt, in 1917. The weight of a Lewis gun was half that of the Vickers, and only two men were needed to carry and operate it. Notice the alarm-rattles on the shelf behind the gunner.

proved so effective that up to 80% of all British casualties to the end of 1915 were thought to have been caused by German machine-guns.

Both armies began the War with just two machine-guns to each battalion. Haig himself at first thought it 'a much over-rated weapon', and even the more imaginative Kitchener decreed initially that four per battalion should be the most allowed, any more being, in his view, a 'luxury'. Trench warfare impelled a radical rethinking. In defence, especially where they were carefully sited in prepared positions which could withstand an artillery barrage, machine-guns could be relied upon to break attacks even if the attackers were in greatly superior numbers.

On 1 July, four and a half German divisions were pitted against thirteen British, yet they inflicted the heaviest losses in the history of British arms. Most casualties occurred near the German wire, where the assaulting troops tended to bunch together and in doing so offered even better targets for the enemy machine-guns. One or two machine-guns on the lip of a mine crater could hold it against a large force of infantry armed only with rifles. Even when smoke screens were laid down to hide the attackers, machine-guns firing on pre-arranged fixed lines could be sure of inflicting serious casualties.

In an attack, their weight was a great disadvantage, though they were often used to fire over the heads of their own advancing troops when the barrage lifted, thereby discouraging the enemy from bringing up his own machine-guns. But the need for lighter, more portable weapons was obvious, and the Lewis gun was chosen for this rôle.

Heavy machine-guns were withdrawn from battalion control at the end of 1915 to form the nucleus of the newly-designated Machine-Gun Corps; eventually this expanded to the point where the ratio of machine-guns per division was at least seven times what it had been at the start of the War. Meanwhile battalions were being equipped with Lewis guns as fast as supplies could be organised. By the time of the Somme every battalion had sixteen Lewis guns, and every brigade possessed its own Machine-Gun Company.

The Lewis gun was essentially an automatic rifle. It could be carried and worked by one man on his own, for it weighed complete only 26½ pounds (12 kg.); but a second man was generally employed as a loader and to carry the ammunition drums, each of which held 47 rounds of .303 calibre. The gun barrel was surrounded by a flanged aluminium radiator to dissipate heat, though in use the weapon soon became too hot to carry without its special asbestos-lined sling. It could fire at a rate of 600 rounds per minute, and twelve drums could be fired off one after the other before the gun seized up through over-heating.

Stoppages were in fact notoriously frequent – over thirty different reasons for stoppages are listed in the gun's official handbook – but mud was by far the commonest cause in practice. Nevertheless, its portability, and the ease and rapidity with which it could be set up on almost any site, made the Lewis gun an extremely valuable addition to the battalion's firepower.

Soon there was at every battalion headquarters an officer whose particular concern was the handling of all matters concerning Lewis guns, from the training of men in their use and maintenance to the siting of Lewis-gun positions in the trench system, and their most effective deployment in an attack. Whenever trenches were to be taken over, the Lewis-gun officer of the relieving battalion would accompany his C.O. on a careful preliminary reconnaissance to decide where best to set up his weapons, which were the battalion's first and most flexible means of defence.

By 1918 each British battalion had acquired no fewer than thirty-two Lewis guns, and more than 130,000 had been manufactured by the end of the War. In July, 1916, the Germans had 11,000 Maxim guns, but in response to the Lewis gun they started to produce their own lightweight weapon, the 25 pound 12 ounce (11.7 kg.) Bergmann.

Some idea of the huge numbers of machine guns in action on the Western front may be gained from the fact that a total of 29,000 of them were captured from the enemy by the victorious British Armies in 1918.

CHAPTER 7

Artillery

In his book *The Wind in the Wires* (Hurst and Blackett, 1923) the fighter pilot Grinnel-Milne tells of how one evening in February, 1916, after he had been captured, he was talking to a fellow-prisoner, a Frenchman. The camp was situated *150 miles* behind the enemy lines. Suddenly the French officer raised his hand. 'Listen!' he said:

> It was scarcely a sound; if it could be compared to anything it was perhaps most like a distant and exceedingly deep-throated growl. But one could feel the concussion more than hear the sound, it was as if the earth itself had shuddered, and as I listened with raised head I swear I saw the branches of a tree tremble . . .
>
> 'That,' said my Frenchman in an awed tone, 'is Verdun. The Boche artillery is busy . . .'

Nothing could exceed the impression of power afforded by such an artillery bombardment. Near to the guns the noise defied description: the earth itself shook, the very air seemed to vibrate. At the receiving end, as death and destruction rained down upon them, men experienced fear in its most primitive and humiliating forms.

There was nothing new in using massed guns to prepare a path down which the infantry could safely advance: the method had been employed by Napoleon in every one of his battles from 1807 onwards. But it was one thing to cut a swathe through a square of infantry with case-shot from a hundred guns brought suddenly into action, and quite a different matter to breach three or four lines of strongly-held, well-constructed trenches with their deep dug-outs and dense wire entanglements. Every increase in the destructive power of high explosive shells had been countered by a

Austrian 30.5 cm. Skoda mortar, used by the Germans in August 1914 to pulverise the Belgian fortresses and open the way to Paris.

A 6-inch gun, unusually lacking in camouflage, firing from a position near Albert in July, 1916, during the Battle of the Somme.

A battery of 60-pounders after being hauled into position near Contalmaison on the Somme. Camouflage-netting will be draped over the scaffolding to hide the guns from enemy aerial observation.

corresponding increase in the strength of the defences. By 1916 the British estimated that three feet of reinforced concrete, or twenty-four feet of clay or loam, gave adequate protection against heavy shells; German dug-outs provided even greater depths of head-cover. For destroying a machine-gun pit or strongpoint more than a hundred 6-inch shells might be needed. The British fired 1,732,873 shells during the 8-day bombardment that preceded their advance on 1 July, 1916, but nevertheless they failed to annihilate the dug-outs and strongpoints of the defenders.

When the War began, neither side had expected to meet with entrenched positions of such strength, although the Germans had taken the trouble to study the problems of siege warfare in preparation for their assault on the forts of Liège and Namur. As early as 1909 the armaments firm of Krupp's at Essen had built for them a monster cannon, 'Big Bertha', of 42 cm. calibre, which could fire an 1800-pound (817 kg.) shell a distance of nine miles. Seven of these cannons were ready by August, 1914, together with the more mobile Austrian-made Skoda 30.5 cm. mortars. Of the twelve forts around Liège only one fell to conventional artillery, but the

The German *Minenwerfer*, a short-range mortar. Used chiefly for destroying trenches, its powerful 50-lb bombs could often be both seen and heard approaching.

remainder surrendered within seventy-two hours of these colossal siege guns being brought into action.

The B.E.F. was well equipped for the period of open warfare which followed. Each of the five Horse Artillery batteries in the Cavalry Division had six 3-inch 13-pounder guns. Each infantry division had four brigades of Royal Field Artillery, a brigade consisting of three batteries, each battery with either six 3.3-inch 18-pounder guns or six 4.5-inch howitzers, making a total of seventy-two guns per division. In addition, each infantry division had a Royal Garrison Artillery battery of four 60-pounder guns of 5-inch calibre.

Australians load a shell into a 9.45-inch trench mortar during the battle of Pozières, August 1916, on the Somme.

France and Germany were similarly equipped, but Germany possessed in addition a large number of field and siege howitzers, giving them a considerable advantage when trench warfare started.

All the British guns were reasonably mobile. The Horse Artillery batteries could, at least in theory, keep pace with the cavalry. The 60-pounders were pulled by teams of dray horses, usually Shires or Clydesdales, even after mechanical means of traction became common. From 1915 onwards, however, new pieces of greatly increased power and weight were brought into use: howitzers of 6-inch, 8-inch, 9.2-inch, 12-inch, and even 15-inch calibre made their appearance on the British front, and these immense weapons required specially-designed lorries for their transport. The heaviest guns, such as the British 12-inch Mark 9, were sometimes railway-mounted to facilitate movement. The problem of how to enable heavy guns to keep up with advances made by infantry over shell-torn country was never satisfactorily solved, which explains why so many offensives ran out of

The German cannon which shelled Paris in 1918 from a distance of over seventy miles. Its shells, weighing 265 lbs., reached a height of twenty-four miles at the top of their trajectory. It was an expensive and inefficient weapon.

A 12-inch howitzer, manned here by an Australian crew. Enormous guns like this usually required railway-mountings. To move them forwards over shell-torn ground was practically impossible.

Canadian gunners loading a 12-inch howitzer in September, 1916.

steam after apparently good beginnings. Fully mobile artillery – in other words, tanks – would, in the next European war, provide the answer.

The function of each piece of artillery depended on its range and on the kind of ammunition employed. Field guns fired either shrapnel or high explosive shells to distances of up to 10,000 yards. A shrapnel shell, the invention of Lieutenant Henry Shrapnel in 1784, contained two or three hundred heavy metal bullets which were scattered by a charge activated by a fuse. Shrapnel was particularly effective against troops in the open, but for destroying trenches howitzers firing high explosive shells were required. These had a range of from 6000 yards, in the case of 4.5-inch field howitzers, to 14,000 yards for the 9.2-inch howitzers brought into service in 1917. Howitzers, like mortars, fire at a steep angle, so that their shells fall almost vertically and can therefore penetrate trenches.

The 6-inch howitzer, firing shells weighing 100 pounds (45 kg.) to a distance of 12,000 yards, became the standard weapon for destroying trenches, buildings, and temporary gun sites. For more distant targets, such as rail-heads, stores

A railway-mounted 9.2-inch gun, concealed in a wood, fires on 1 July, 1916. Because of manufacturing errors, premature explosions in the breech were not uncommon; and many shells fired from British guns on 1 July turned out to be 'duds'.

dumps, crossroads, and assembly areas, the 60-pound gun was ideal. Bridges and strongly fortified gun emplacements were unlikely to be significantly damaged except by heavier howitzers of 8-inch calibre and upwards.

Trench warfare saw the reintroduction of an old weapon, the mortar – a short-range howitzer. The German *Minenwerfer* had a range of 450 yards and fired a 50-pound (23 kg.) bomb which could destroy a section of trench. Nicknamed 'Moaning Minnies' by the British, these missiles rose to a height of about 500 feet before descending steeply, emitting a characteristic whine and permitting, occasionally, the section of trench in the line of fire to be cleared in time. The corresponding British weapon was the Stokes mortar, a model of simple, effective design. The standard 3-inch Stokes mortar proved so light, handy, and efficient that it was often used as a close-support weapon in an attack, as well as routinely in the trenches. Another very successful British mortar was the Livens gas projector, which was used at

1 July, 1916, on the Somme. The German dug-outs were sometimes so deep that they could even withstand the enormous explosive power of this howitzer's 12-inch shells.

Beaumont Hamel in the autumn of 1916 to fire large numbers of drums of gas into Y-Ravine and into the fortress itself.

At the other end of the scale to the trench mortar was the German long-range howitzer which began to bombard Paris on 23 March, 1918. It fired its 265-pound (120 kg.) 5.3-inch shell a distance of more than seventy miles, but was insufficiently accurate to be more than a weapon of terror, and was therefore used only against unprotected civilians. Only 203 rounds were fired altogether, the wear on the gun's inner tube being so great that it had to be changed every sixty rounds. The gun was of no tactical significance, and absorbed resources of material and labour that might have been better employed elsewhere.

In the case of such extremely long-range guns, the inaccuracy of aim was the result of special factors such as the rapid wearing of the gun-barrel, unknown weather conditions near the target area, and even the effect of the earth's

The crew of an 18-pounder stripped for action in the battle for Pozières Ridge, July, 1916. Pozières finally fell to the 1st Australian Division after an appallingly costly struggle.

rotation during the missile's lengthy flight. But all artillery weapons needed skill in handling if they were to give their best results. As a rule the German gunners were masters of their art, and their British counterparts had some bitter lessons to learn before they acquired similar expertise. The enormous expansion of the artillery – the heavy artillery alone increased from 36 batteries on 1 January, 1915, to 191 batteries on 1 July, 1916 – meant that few gun-crews went into action on the Somme adequately trained, and far too many senior artillery officers lacked experience of high command. Not surprisingly, the artillery preparation for the Somme offensive was a disastrous failure.

Not only inexperience was to blame, however. Much of the ammunition issued by British factories in 1916 was poorly made, either failing to explode or doing so prematurely. Two 9.2-inch howitzers were put out of action, one on 1 July, by explosions in the breech. Unexploded 8-inch howitzer shells littered the battlefield: 'duds' are still, seventy years later, being turned up by the ploughs of French farmers. Sixty-

The cheerful crew of a 6-inch howitzer in action on the Somme, July 1916. This gun, christened by its crew 'The Vimy Queen', has been moved south from Vimy to take part in the Somme offensive.

pounder shells averaged two premature explosions for every thousand fired, and the 4.5-inch howitzer batteries became known as 'suicide clubs' because of the frequency of such extremely dangerous incidents.

The guns themselves, subjected to heavier usage than ever before, began to reveal serious defects. The springs of the 18-pounders, designed to return the gun-barrel to the firing position after each recoil, either broke or lost strength, and spares were unobtainable. Some worn-out gun-barrels ought to have been discarded, but the replacements offered were found to be of such inferior metal that they were no better than the original pieces.

However, the principal cause of the British artillery's poor showing on 1 July lay less in defective material than in faulty intelligence work and lack of liaison with the forward troops. The existence of those deep dug-outs which sheltered the German defenders during the long bombardment should have been known at General Headquarters level, and not have come to everyone there as a complete surprise.

75 h.p. Holt tractors hauling 8-inch howitzers into 'Death Valley' on the Somme, 1916. Notice the men taking cover as a shell bursts near them (left of picture). Through this valley had to pass many of the British troops on their way to and from the front line. It was under constant observation from enemy balloons, and earned for itself a particularly evil reputation.

Battalions should not have had to advance against inadequately cut wire, and especially not against wire which was well known – but only at infantry battalion level – to be still intact. In any case, it should have been realised that wire-cutting was best done by field artillery, since heavy guns merely added to the problems of the infantry by creating huge shell-craters across their line of advance.

Above all, the artillery timetable on 1 July was too inflexible, and made no allowance for the inevitable delays, hold-ups, and unforeseen changes of circumstance of the battlefield. Troops found themselves pinned down in No-Man's-Land by unsubdued German field guns, while their own barrage moved off into the distance, in strict observance of orders, when it could have been far better employed engaging those enemy guns.

Such criticism, of course, has the inestimable benefit of hindsight. What the artillery attempted at the start of the Somme offensive was something new to British arms. Considering the doubtful quality of many of their weapons, the defects of their ammunition, and the lack of experience of so many of their officers, the gun-crews may be judged to have performed remarkably well.

And the lessons of 1 July were not wasted. From then on,

accuracy of fire improved with the introduction of more sophisticated techniques of sound-location and flash-spotting. 'Ranging' involved straddling a target with shots fired successively closer and closer on instructions from a forward observation officer on the ground or an observer in the air. But improved sound-location (using 'hot-wire' microphones and parabolic receivers) and flash-spotting (pin-pointing enemy gun-flashes by accurate triangulation) enabled the position of enemy batteries to be fixed, and guns trained precisely on them, without first subjecting them to observed fire: they could then be taken by surprise and destroyed before enemy guns could retaliate. Such 'predicted' fire, as it was called, became an important artillery technique, but it was not available until after the close of the Battle of the Somme.

Like the 'creeping' barrage, gas shelling was introduced during that battle, using at first both guns and ammunition supplied by the French. Gas shells, being lighter than shrapnel or high explosive shells, needed special range tables. For maximum effect they required either a very still day, or at most a light wind blowing towards the enemy positions.

Before the War ended, artillery battles dwarfing those of the Somme had taken place at Arras (April, 1917), where 963 heavy guns were in action, and at Messines the following month, where over 2000 guns, 756 of them heavy, were deployed along a nine-mile front. Nothing the British artillery attempted, however, was to compare with the hurricane bombardment which the Germans unleashed against the British Fifth and Third Armies at 4.30 a.m. on the morning of 21 March, 1918.

Colonel Bruchmüller (punningly nicknamed Durchbruch-Müller – 'Breakthrough-Müller' – by the Germans) had secretly assembled a vast array of more than 4000 guns of every calibre for his opening barrage, each detail of which he had meticulously planned and orchestrated. Using only 'predicted' fire, for although the sun rose at 6 a.m. a dense fog continued all morning to envelop the battlefield, he first of all saturated the British forward headquarters and battery positions with an intense concentration of gas shells. At intervals high explosive shells were added, then more gas shells of various kinds to confuse the opposition, then still more high explosive shells. Meanwhile the British redoubts in the zone nearest the enemy were swept with devastating fire from field batteries and trench mortars, and soon the thinly-held British trenches behind the redoubts were completely obliterated. After five hours of such continuous preparation, the way was clear for the German infantry, who swarmed out of their assembly trenches and advanced across No-Man's-Land behind a devastating 'creeping' barrage.

At the time it seemed like the apotheosis of the gun as an instrument of war – as if the ultimate invincible weapon had been forged. Yet within fifteen days the advance, failing to maintain momentum, petered out with not one of its objectives reached. Despite the efforts of its artillery, the German High Command lost that battle of Amiens, although never in all the years of trench warfare had the German Army come so close to the realisation of its dream of snatching victory on the Western Front.

CHAPTER 8

The Fog of War

In that searingly honest record of trench life, *The War the Infantry Knew* (edited anonymously; published by King, 1938), there occurs the following paragraph:

> At the beginning of the morning attack the enemy barrage cut the wires. The barrage smoke made lamp signalling impossible, even if adequate preparation had been made for it. The wireless set provided was for transmission only, so it was not known if messages were being received. The supply of runners was soon exhausted and was not replaced. At noon I went to Brigade to report the futility of it all.

The exasperation felt by this officer on 20 July, 1916, unable to learn how his men were faring in their attack, and without the means to communicate information which might have helped them, was the result of circumstances by no means unique. Indeed it was typical of much of the fighting of World War 1 that the troops, once they passed beyond their own front line, seemed to enter a region of limbo where they felt as cut off from the rest of the Army as if they had been suddenly translated to another planet. The 'fog of war', which in the past had been a literal reference to the smoke from cannon and musket that hung over a battlefield, now took on an abstract and more sinister meaning. From the moment that an attack was launched, whole battalions – the Newfoundland Regiment at Beaumont Hamel on 1 July is but one example among many – could face virtual extinction without their divisional headquarters even being aware that they were in difficulties.

The situation had no precedent. Hitherto, all great battles had been fought in the actual presence of the opposing commanders, whose control over the course of events was

Men of the Royal Engineers carry reels of telephone wire up to the front line. Not a shred of vegetation remains in the devastated landscape.

manifestly supreme. Neither Bruce at Bannockburn, nor Napoleon at Austerlitz, nor Wellington at Waterloo was ever farther than a short gallop from the most outlying of his forces. He could follow the progress of the battle not only from the reports arriving by the minute, but also by merely using his eyes; and he could amend his plans, call up his reserves, re-direct fire, and improvise new tactics exactly as the occasion seemed to demand. The entire responsibility was his, and all that his junior officers had to do was to make sure that orders were carried out. Now, however, here on the Western front from 1915 onwards, battles on a scale dwarfing those of the past were being fought, yet never had commanders been so frustrated in their efforts to retain control over what happened on the battlefield; nor, as a corollary to that, had the need been so pressing for junior officers to be men of real intelligence and enterprise.

When World War 2 came to be fought, the situation had changed again: thanks to improvements in short-wave radio

A Royal Garrison Artillery forward observation post in a shell-hole. A message is being passed back to the guns in Morse Code by means of a Fullerphone telegraph.

transmission, a Commander could once more keep in close touch with his formations throughout a battle. In the great setpiece encounters of World War 1, however, success time and again proved elusive, not least because of this simple lack of a workable inter-communication system.

Wireless had in fact been in use in the field from August 1915 onwards, but the apparatus of that period needed heavy accumulator batteries and a large cumbersome aerial, making it quite unsuitable for work farther forward than Brigade Headquarters. Smaller, less vulnerable sets were subsequently available down to battalion level. They were never very reliable, and were tedious to use, since every message could be picked up on enemy receiving sets and most had therefore to be coded before transmission. As a back-up to cable telegraph and telephone, wireless was of value, but its potential lay in the future.

Cable telephone communication had played an important

The beauty of a battlefield at night: flares and rockets weave patterns in the darkness over No-Man's-Land. Photographed near Thiepval, on the Somme, 7 August, 1916.

part in previous campaigns, and the Army had been able to provide a useful Signals service from the start of hostilities. Telegraphed signals in Morse code had been used as far back as the Crimean War of 1853-56; their value was well established. Strangely enough, in the first weeks of the War the German Army appeared to overlook the importance of maintaining good communications. As their cavalry squadrons swept southwards into France in August, 1914, they deliberately set about destroying telephones and telephone lines. The armies of the German right wing were later to pay dearly at the Battle of the Marne for this short-sighted piece of vandalism.

A field telephone could be set up anywhere in a matter of minutes with just a reel of cable and a handset. It was simple to use and technically uncomplicated; repairs could be made by anyone of modest manual skill. Its one great weakness was the vulnerability of its cable to damage. Shellfire and heavy traffic severed cables laid along the ground, and wires suspended from telegraph poles were snapped by shrapnel. By 1915 it was becoming necessary to bury all cables near the front line in special trenches. At first 18 inches down was considered sufficient, but as the War went on and firepower rose, the depth had to be correspondingly increased. By the time of the Battle of the Somme, the Germans were relying on a 6-foot 'bury' for cables at the bottom of a fire trench, but they preferred a 10-foot bury for cables across open ground.

British orders on 1 April, 1916 specified a depth of 'not less than 6 feet', which it was calculated would protect the cable against as many as fifty direct hits, provided that the shells were less than 8-inch calibre.

The labour involved in digging trenches for cables was prodigious, especially when it was found advisable to bury them as far back as divisional headquarters. Any change in the location of headquarters, as necessarily occurred in the course of a battle like the Somme, entailed a whole new digging operation. Eventually a more flexible system was devised, with lateral connections and deeply buried junction-boxes. The new system had the great advantage of helping to overcome one problem which had beset communications from the earliest days of trench warfare: how to maintain contact during a battle with the units on one's flanks.

The cables in the front-line trenches were of course particularly susceptible to damage, and were therefore installed in duplicate or even triplicate. Forty thousand miles of cable were issued by the Ordnance Depot in Calais in 1915, but more than that was used in 1916 in the massive preparations for the Somme offensive.

In June, 1915, a serious new problem arose when it became apparent that telephone messages from forward positions were somehow being intercepted by the enemy. One cause was quickly identified: the opposing trenches were by then so close to each other in places that by using an earth induction receiver the Germans had been able to tap the British circuits. The obvious solution was to change from

A pigeon is released from a forward trench. In a few minutes it will be back at its home loft, and the message fastened to its leg will be passed to Intelligence at Divisional Headquarters.

Each of these birds has lost a leg as a result of a war wound. Whether they received war pensions is not recorded.

alternating to interrupted direct current; but there were other sources of leaks – for example, damage to the insulation around cables – which were less easily eliminated. A German listening post intercepted a message in the early hours of 1 July, 1916, which gave clear warning of the impending attack. It had been telephoned from Brigade to forward British units who, when they later entered enemy trenches at Ovillers, were disgusted to find the same message translated into German and prominently displayed on the wall of a dug-out. Thereafter, some deliberately faulty circuits were retained for the purpose of 'leaking' misleading information to the enemy; but elsewhere security was tightened, jamming devices were introduced, and towards the end of that year a new instrument called the Fullerphone, which could not be easily tapped, was brought into service.

One problem continued to defy solution: how to maintain efficient inter-communication during a battle. Sooner or later – but usually sooner – every cable in the battle area would be severed; and even while the cables remained intact only snatches of a telephone conversation were audible above the din of the barrage.

The paramount need for the side under attack was to alert its own artillery, so that a counter-barrage could be directed on to the enemy's trenches and on to the sector of No-Man's-Land across which his attack was being launched. The Germans evolved a simple but effective system using rockets, which not only could be seen from a great distance but were immune from the hazards affecting cables. Different colours and combinations supplied coded information to artillery units far to the rear, who were able to respond immediately. The rocket flares were bright enough to be seen in daylight; at night, in an active sector, the sky took on a weird beauty as lights of all colours rose and fell in the darkness. Both sides made use of rocket flares, but the Germans came to depend on them more than did the British. The limitations of the system were not fully appreciated until the successful British assault on Beamont Hamel in November, 1916.

Mobile loft for carrier pigeons on the Somme, October 1916. The sign on the loft reads 'Out of Bounds': it was not unknown for pigeons to end up supplementing the diet of hungry troops.

For troops who were attacking, communication problems multiplied from the moment the men left their trenches. There was no shortage of solutions: every conceivable means of transmitting signals was tried out during the course of the battles of the Somme; none was found to be without its drawbacks. Telephone cables which had been reeled out across No-Man's-Land seldom survived for long in the storm of shell and shrapnel. Signalling with flags, white discs, or electric torches merely drew down enemy fire. Flares and rockets were sometimes effective, but the information they could transmit was limited.

Aircraft were used extensively on 1 July to follow the progress of the advancing infantry, who replied with coloured flares to the aviator's blast on his Klaxon horn, the pre-arranged signal for 'Where are you?' The airman noted the position on his map, which he later dropped at brigade or divisional headquarters. He kept in touch with the artillery by wireless, and he could signal to troops on the ground by lamp or Very pistol, a device which fired an intensely luminous flare. On 1 July some infantrymen in each battalion carried on their backs small metal mirrors which flashed in the sunlight and enabled observers to follow their progress; unfortunately, the mirrors also revealed the wearer's whereabouts to the enemy.

Message-carrying rockets, with a range of more than a mile, were occasionally employed by the British, but, as the writer of an interesting article on the subject explains in the *Encyclopaedia Britannica* (14th Edition, 1929), a much more reliable form of aerial transport was the carrier pigeon:

> . . .they might be delayed by darkness, chased by hawks, lost in the smoke and uproar or killed in crossing a barrage, but they made their lofts on the whole with remarkable regularity and sometimes showed a pathetic courage. More than one reached its loft wounded and died as it alighted, and one such in the French Army was officially decorated for valour.

By 1918 there were 20,000 birds in the pigeon service, and 90,000 men had been trained in their management.

When all else failed, there remained those few individuals upon whom communications in the maelstrom of battle would ultimately depend: the company and battalion runners. Chosen from the best and steadiest in the battalion, these were men whose physical powers of endurance had to be matched by a dogged tenacity of purpose. Some seemed to lead charmed lives as they dodged from crater to crater across the fire-swept waste, emerging breathless but cheerful from a hail of bullets through which it was hard to imagine anyone could pass unscathed. Few runners survived to record for later generations the full story of their exploits. Many hundreds vanished without trace in the wilderness of No-Man's-Land, becoming perhaps the anonymous subject of that bleak phrase which crops up so often in the *Official History:* 'No runner could get through . . .' Some, like Private Miller of the 7th Battalion, the 'King's Own', were mortally wounded, but refused to die until they had delivered their precious messages.

If no runner could get through, then the last hope of a unit which was running short of ammunition, or whose retreat was about to be cut off, or which was being shelled to destruction, would begin to wither and fade.

One runner who did 'get through' was Drummer William Kenny of the 2nd Gordon Highlanders, who won the Victoria Cross at First Ypres not only for rescuing wounded men on five occasions while under very heavy fire, but also for twice saving machine-guns from capture by the enemy, and not least for conveying 'on numerous occasions . . . urgent messages under very dangerous circumstances over fire-swept ground.'

In such a heroic mould was many a battalion runner fashioned.

CHAPTER 9

Poison Gas

After the capture of Courcelette, in which tanks were used for the first time, one of the rank-and-file German prisoners remarked bitterly that what he had just witnessed was 'not war but bloody butchery'.

What is and what is not considered fair in war – as in love – clearly varies with one's viewpoint. Great indignation was expressed by Britain when the Germans first used poison gas, which had been banned under the terms of an international agreement signed by all the Great Powers (except the United States) in 1899; but this disapproval did not deter the Allies from immediately resorting to the same weapon, and in Britain only a few voices were raised in protest.

From the German point of view, poison gas had seemed at first glance a natural war-winner. The chemical industry before the War had been dominated by Germany, which possessed more trained chemists and better, as well as larger, manufacturing plant than any other nation. Many toxic gases were known: one, chlorine, was readily produced in large quantities and was particularly suitable for use on the battlefield.

Discovered in 1774 by the Swedish chemist Scheele, chlorine was used in many industrial processes, as well as in the large-scale purification of water ('chlorination'). It is a greenish-yellow gas, heavier than air, with a strong, characteristic smell – the smell familiar to anyone who has visited a public swimming-pool. In low concentration the gas is completely harmless, but if the concentration is raised, the irritating effect on the respiratory tract increases until eventually the lining of the lungs and breathing tubes pours out so much fluid that the victim may drown in his own

The first gas attack was at Ypres on 22 April, 1915. Here men of the 2nd Argyll & Sutherland Highlanders are wearing the primitive cotton-pad gas-masks issued to them on 3 May.

secretions. A concentration of 2.5mg. per litre in air causes death within a few minutes.

This was the gas released by the Germans on 22 April, 1915 against the northern perimeter of the Ypres salient. There the line was being held by the French 45th Division, consisting of Zouaves (members of a tribe of Algerian Berbers) and three African battalions; the French 87th (Territorial) Division – rather elderly reservists; the 1st Canadian Division; and the 28th, 29th, and 5th British divisions.

At 5 p.m., on receipt of a signal from an observation balloon that the wind direction was favourable, the gas cylinder taps were opened along the German front line. Like a dense yellow fog, hugging the contours of the ground, the gas drifted slowly across the narrow divide of No-Man's-Land and began to filter down into the trenches occupied by the French Colonial troops. What followed was graphically described by Sir John French:

'DUCK YER NUT' is the message on this gas-alarm bell in a trench at Beaumont Hamel. It is December 1916: snow has fallen, and the sentry is well-padded.

> The effect of the gas was so overwhelming that the whole of the positions occupied by the French Divisions was rendered incapable of any resistance. It was impossible at first to realise what had actually happened. Fumes and smoke obscured everything. Hundreds of men were thrown into a stupor, and after an hour the whole position had to be abandoned together with fifty guns.

General Sir William Robertson, then Chief of the General Staff, showed little sympathy for the behaviour of the poor Zouaves. He commented sourly: 'I think there must have been something invigorating about that gas. I am sure I could not have run all the way from Ypres to Dunkirk without a tonic'.

What is extraordinary is that the Germans failed completely to exploit the opportunity offered. The very success of the new weapon seemed to throw them, as much as the defenders, into confusion. By the time their infantry had penetrated the four-mile gap left in the line by the

Australian troops wearing box-type respirators with rubber face-masks and goggles pose (with fixed bayonets) for the official photographer in a trench near Ypres; September 1917.

Zouaves' disappearance, the Canadian and British divisions had rallied sufficiently to counter further advances. Nor were the German infantry at all eager to move into the lingering gas-cloud, although most of them were equipped with respirators. Darkness fell with their front line pushed forward a matter of two miles, but by dawn the Canadians and British had firmly closed the gap.

Over the next five weeks a vicious battle was fought out, with more gas discharges and further small reductions in the size of the Salient. But nowhere did the line again break and Ypres itself remained in Allied hands.

The day after the first gas attack Sir John French sent to the War Office an urgent request for suitable respirators. The earliest consisted simply of a pad of cotton soaked in a solution of bicarbonate of soda, which neutralised the chlorine. Taped over the mouth, and used with a nose-clip, the pad gave some protection but so restricted the breathing

A Seaforth Highlander on gas-sentry duty beside his compressed-air alarm horn. Photographed near Arras on 23 October, 1917.

that physical exertion was almost impossible. These first primitive gas-masks were produced by women in Britain in response to a public appeal from Lord Kitchener himself. Within a matter of days every man in the B.E.F. had been provided with a degree of protection. Much more efficient was a respirator in which the air breathed in was filtered through activated charcoal and soda lime. Such respirators took time to manufacture, but by July, 1915, the whole B.E.F. was supplied with a helmet respirator which had an impregnated bag and a celluloid window. The familiar box respirators were issued at the time of the Battle of the Somme in 1916.

Other methods of combating gas attacks were investigated, but none was an improvement on the respirator. Sir Hiram Maxim, inventor of the Maxim machine-gun, suggested firing incendiary bombs into the approaching gas-cloud which, being heated, would rise out of harm's way. Less rational was the hand-held fan devised by a Mrs. Hertha Ayrton, who claimed that it could be used to drive the gas back towards the enemy. She personally financed the manufacture of 150,000 Ayrton fans; the troops cynically used them for fuel.

British plans for retaliation began almost at once, but progress was hampered by a dearth of suitably trained chemists and the scarcity of large-scale chemical plants. In the whole country only one firm, the Kestner-Kellner Alkali Company, had the technology for liquefying chlorine gas. Even the gas cylinders had to be specially manufactured, and the first models were found to leak dangerously at the joints. Special piping had to be procured for projecting the gas over No-Man's-Land, and great difficulty was experienced in making these pipes leak-proof. The standard of British workmanship may be judged from the fact that the spanners used to turn on the gas were of such soft metal that they split apart in use. Some valve-nuts were found to have been made round instead of square, and so could not be turned at all when the cylinders reached the trenches.

But occasionally the British showed foresight and imagination. They foresaw that the poisonous gas phosgene would also be suitable for use in warfare, and set about adapting the standard British respirator so that it was effective against both chlorine and phosgene. For years, phosgene had been used by German chemists in the manufacture of dyes. Like chlorine it irritates the respiratory tract, but phosgene is much more dangerous and can kill suddenly by a delayed effect, sometimes as long as forty-eight hours after exposure to apparently trivial doses. It was in fact used by the Germans against the British on 19 December, 1915, north-east of Ypres, in the form of gas-shells. The Germans there had expected an easy victory, and were surprised to discover that the British had gas-masks equipped to deal with the new gas. Even so, 120 men died out of more than 1000 gas-casualties. The protection afforded by a gas-mask is only relative: a very high concentration of gas will quickly render any ordinary gas-mask useless, and quite moderate levels of concentration can, if continued long

All the equipment for a Livens mortar-bomb projector, set out in a teaching demonstration behind the lines. Each bomb weighed about 60 lbs and could contain either poison gas, or a smoke mixture, or an incendiary liquid.

enough, have the same effect.

The British first used poison gas at Loos on 25 September, 1915. The battle illustrates only too clearly the vices of the new weapon.

Smoke as well as gas was to be released – the former partly to obscure the advance of the infantry, and partly to eke out the gas, which was still in short supply. A front of no less than six miles had been chosen for the discharge of the chlorine. By dawn on the 25th, 5500 gas cylinders and 11,000 smoke candles were safely in position along the front line trenches. All that was lacking was a favourable breeze.

Fig. 2 shows wind-roses for each month in the Loos area, compiled from readings taken between 1905 and 1914. (This diagram, and a very detailed account of the use made of chemical weapons in the War, can be found in the monograph *"Gas!"*, by C. Foulkes; Blackwood, 1934.) The length of each radius represents the frequency of surface

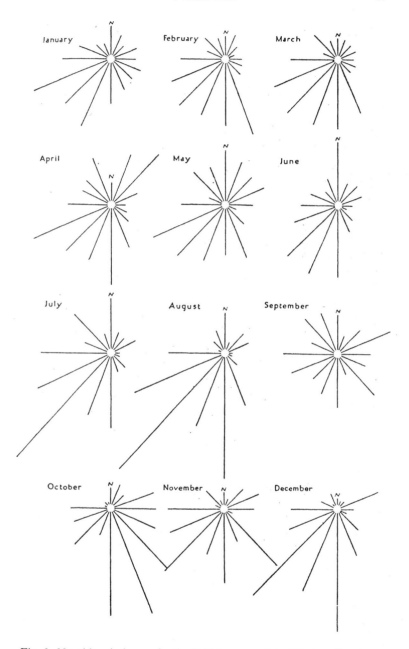

Fig. 2. Monthly wind roses for the British sector of the Western Front.

winds of between 4 and 15 m.p.h. blowing *from* that particular direction. As might be expected, south-westerly winds predominate, and winds from the quarter between south and west are more common that winds from the other quarters. (Similar wind patterns were to be found all along the Western Front, favouring the Allies' gas attacks, but handicapping their aviators.) September and October, however, are exceptions to this rule: in those months the wind in fact blows more often from eastern than from western quarters. Failure of the wind to blow effectively towards the enemy's trenches on 25 September, 1915 was the main reason why the battle was as good as lost in the first hour.

The gas was scheduled to be discharged at dawn. Forty minutes later, the infantry would begin their advance.

All through the night the forty officers of the Special Gas Company sent in telephone reports on wind speed and direction to Haig's headquarters six miles behind the lines. Earlier, conditions had looked promising; but towards dawn the wind veered and dropped, especially on the left of the front. It was too late by then, apparently, to cancel the attack. Punctually at 5.50 a.m. the cylinder-taps were opened all along the front. Foulkes described the initial picture thus:

> The first aeroplane report that came in a few minutes later was to the effect that the gas cloud was rolling steadily over towards the German lines; and from the top of the tall wooden tower which had been specially constructed as an observation post in the château grounds an awe-inspiring spectacle was visible, the whole countryside to the front, as far as the eye could reach, being enveloped in what appeared to be a vast prairie conflagration.

Soon, however, it became clear that in many places the gas was hindering rather than helping the attackers. For example, the 2nd Gordon Highlanders in the famous 7th Division ran into gas and lost many men, though Piper Munro encouraged the remainder with his indomitable piping to continue their assault. Several Gas Officers, correctly assessing the wind conditions as unfavourable, at first declined to open up their cylinders. Divisional Headquarters overruled them, and some battalions were, as a result, poisoned even before they left their trenches. Others, suffering badly from the effects of their own gas, but still determined to take part, arrived in front of the German wire to be greeted with fire from unaffected enemy machine-gunners. Inevitably, some cylinders were burst open by the enemy's counter-barrage, causing serious and even fatal injuries among the closely-packed troops.

Nevertheless some divisions, notably the 9th and the 15th, did remarkably well at Loos. These were New Army divisions lately arrived in France, and their zeal and panache surprised even their own officers. It was a portent of the future. But in general the Loos offensive was a bungled affair, a costly failure for which the misuse of the poison gas was much to blame. Of the twelve divisions taking part, the 9th and the 15th – both Scottish – sustained the most casualties: 5868 and 6668 respectively.

Obviously what was needed for the effective exploitation of the new weapon was a method of firing the gas containers into the enemy positions from a distance. For this purpose the newly-invented Stokes mortar was to prove ideal, but because of manufacturing delays gas-shells were not available for it until 1917 – too late for the Somme offensive. However, in that battle gas-bombs were fired from 2-inch trench mortars into Thiepval and Beaumont Hamel, and on 28 October 135 40-pound bombs filled with phosgene were projected by the new Livens mortar into Y-Ravine south of Beaumont Hamel and into the stronghold of Serre. Before then, almost all poison-gas shells used by the British had been fired from borrowed French batteries.

On 11 November, 1916, Beaumont Hamel was deluged with 4-inch mortar bombs containing a lachrymatory gas, and once again Y-Ravine was bombarded with gas-drums. These gas attacks on Beaumont Hamel contributed

Livens projectors in position before camouflaging. Up to 1000 bombs could be fired within seconds from such emplacements, producing a very high concentration of gas at the target area. The maximum range was 3000 yards.

significantly to the success of the great assault on that fortress on 13 November.

As the War went on, many other toxic substances were tried out by both sides: prussic acid, chloropicrin, various arsenical compounds, and dichlorethyl sulphide ('mustard gas'), as well as a whole range of non-lethal but highly incapacitating lachrymators (tear-gases).

Mustard gas – the substance used by the Iraquis against Iranian troops in 1984 – was introduced by the Germans in July, 1917. Its effects are particularly loathsome. The inhaled vapour inflames the whole respiratory tract, causing choking and asphyxia, while the slightest contact of the liquid with the skin results in an intensely painful burn. Large areas of skin may slough off, leaving raw wounds which take many months to heal. Permanent blindness may result from splashes in the eyes.

Mustard gas came to be used particularly where a portion of ground was to be denied to attacking troops, or where it was hoped to prevent reserve forces from coming to the aid of defenders. Ground contaminated with mustard gas remained dangerous for many weeks.

Contrary to popular belief, poison gas as a weapon was less lethal than bullets or shells. Of the 181,000 British gas-casualties, 6000 died – about 3.3%. The mortality rate for all other battle injuries was 25%. Reliable figures are not available for German casualties, but it is unlikely that their percentage mortality was very different.

Chemical warfare set the Allies a particularly taxing industrial problem. Once again they found themselves at a technical disadvantage, ill-equipped in both knowledge and materials. Colossal efforts had to be made, both in the factories and on the battlefield, before the enemy could be met on anything like equal terms. Once again, the ordinary soldier was called upon to pay the price for national unpreparedness.

CHAPTER 10

Tanks

Poison gas was the German solution to the deadlock in the trenches. The British solution was the tank.

The problem which the tank attempted to answer was threefold: how could the crossing of No-Man's-Land be rendered less hazardous; how could the enemy's barbed wire be effectively cut or flattened; and how could a sufficiently wide breach be made in the enemy's trench system for the long-delayed 'break-out' to become a reality?

Several ingenious minds arrived more or less simultaneously at the same answer, but it was Lieutenant-Colonel E.D. Swinton, of the Royal Engineers, who possessed the energy and conviction to carry the idea to a practical conclusion. He found a powerful ally in Winston Churchill, whose letter to Prime Minister Asquith on 5 January, 1915 combines an admirable grasp of the technicalities with a shrewd insight into the tactical possibilities – as well as displaying a characteristic impatience with bureaucratic delay:

> It is extraordinary that the Army in the Field and the War Office should have allowed nearly three months of trench warfare to progress without addressing their minds to its special problems.
>
> The present war has revolutionised all military theories about the field of fire. The power of the rifle is so great that 100 yards is held sufficient to stop any rush, and in order to avoid the severity of the artillery fire, trenches are often dug on the reverse slope of positions, or a short distance in the rear of villages, woods, or other obstacles. The consequence is that the war has become a short range instead of a long range war as was expected, and opposing trenches get ever closer together for mutual safety from each other's artillery fire.

The question to be solved is not therefore the long attack over a carefully prepared glacis of former times, but the actual getting across of 100 or 200 yards of open space and wire entanglements. All this was apparent more than two months ago, but no steps have been taken and no preparation made. It would be quite easy in a short time to fit up a number of steam tractors with small armoured shelters, in which men and machine guns could be placed, which would be bulletproof. Used at night they would not be affected by artillery fire to any extent. The caterpillar system would enable trenches to be crossed quite easily, and the weight of the machine would destroy all wire entanglements. Forty or fifty of these engines prepared secretly and brought into position at nightfall could advance quite certainly into the enemy's trenches, smashing away all obstructions and sweeping the trenches with their machine-gun fire and with grenades thrown out of the top. They would then make so many *points d'appui* for the British supporting infantry to rush forward to attack the second line of trenches. The cost would be small. If the experiment did not answer, what harm would be done? An obvious measure of prudence would have been to have started something like this two months ago. It should certainly be done now.

Churchill's vision of a fleet of steam-driven, bullet-proof troop-carriers lumbering into action at night across No-Man's-Land – guns blazing, grenades being hurled out of the top – is splendidly Wellsian. The reality, when tanks eventually took the field on 15 September, 1916, was scarcely less impressive.

The designers had taken each aspect of the problem in turn and produced a logical solution. For example, the best means of negotiating very rough ground was to use caterpillar tracks, so these were incorporated into the design at an early stage. Machines so equipped had been in use for several years in the forests of California, moving heavy loads across difficult terrain. The wide tread of their caterpillar tracks, by spreading the weight over a large area, allowed them to

'Clan Leslie', a Mark 1 tank, on its way to the battle of Flers-Courcelette, 15 September 1916, where the tanks made their début. The two huge rear wheels, designed to assist steering, were discarded in later models.

work on soft ground into which vehicles with ordinary wheels would sink. Transverse ridges on the tracks, comparable with the tread pattern on a modern tyre, gave a better grip on slippery ground and improved the vehicle's ability to climb slopes.

The specification drawn up by the War Office stipulated that the vehicle should be able to cross a ten-foot-wide trench. This led to the characteristic lozenge-shaped profile of World War 1 tanks (see fig. 3). When a vertical line through the tank's centre of mass falls within the trench (fig. 3, b) the front of the tank will begin to tilt downwards. This brings the forward-facing portions of its track up against the farther edge of the trench (fig. 3, c), so that the vehicle can pull itself back into a horizontal position (fig. 3, d). As the tank continues forward, its centre of mass falls beyond the trench, and the hinder end of the tank cannot then tilt downwards (fig. 3, e). If the trench is ten feet wide, the vehicle obviously needs to be approximately twice that in length. The Mark 1 tanks, the first to go into action, were in fact 26½ feet long, almost 14 feet wide, and about 8 feet in height.

On the first tanks the armour-plating was up to half an inch (12 mm.) thick in front of the driver, and not less than

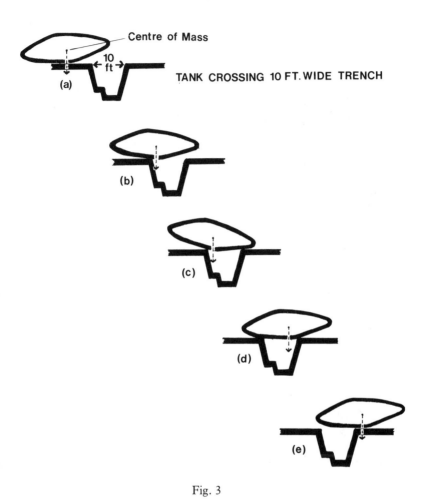

Centre of Mass

(a)

TANK CROSSING 10 FT. WIDE TRENCH

(b)

(c)

(d)

(e)

Fig. 3

6mm. thick over the roof and belly. That thickness of steel gave them complete protection against standard German bullets, but added enormously to their weight. With limited horsepower available, the designers faced an awkward choice: which should be given priority – the vehicle's speed, or the safety of the crew? They chose the latter, and the Mark 1, weighing a colossal twenty-eight tons, eventually crawled into battle at a ponderous 3.7 m.p.h. in top gear. Across the sort of ground found on the battlefield of the Somme it seldom

A carrier pigeon being released from the port-hole of a tank. Communications with the outside world posed a severe problem for tank crews, and in battle the tank commander usually had to make his own decisions on which targets to attack.

A Mark 1 'male' tank crosses a trench on its way to Thiepval, 25 September 1916. Its armament includes two 6-pounder guns for annihilating machine-gun posts. The structure on the roof supports wire-netting to deflect grenades.

What purports to be a dramatic picture of a cowed German emerging from beneath a tank is actually posed and phoney. This tank was lying derelict in a shell-hole, having been destroyed in the battle of Flers-Courcelette, when an enterprising photographer spotted it as a subject for tongue-in-cheek propaganda.

exceeded 0.5 m.p.h. Although the decision to put armour before speed was probably correct, a slow target is easier to hit than a fast-moving one, and many tanks fell victim to German field-guns.

Two versions of the Mark 1 were produced, known as 'male' or 'female' depending on the type of armament carried. The 'male' tank had two 6-pounder guns, each with 160 rounds of ammunition, and four Hotchkiss machine-guns, each with 1500 rounds. The 'female' tank carried machine-guns only: five Vickers, each with 4800 rounds, and one Hotchkiss with 3000 rounds. 'Male' tanks were to be used chiefly against machine-gun posts, 'females' against personnel. These weapons were housed in 'sponsons' – armoured projections on the sides of the hull – fitted with ports through which each gun could be individually aimed and fired.

The Mark 1 had a crew of eight: an officer and seven men,

A tank at Flers on 17 September, 1916. The officer is in shirtsleeves. The man relaxing on top of the tank is using a field telephone. The others – to judge from their glum expressions – have just been told that their next job is to dig the huge machine out of the bank in which it has got itself stuck.

three of whom steered the monster. From the main two-speed gearbox, controlled by the driver, the power was transmitted to a second gearbox on each half-shaft. Each secondary gearbox required an operator, who could control with a hand lever the speed at which the driving sprockets in the rear of the chassis turned the caterpillar tracks. With the left track running and the other track stationary the tank turned sharply to the right, and vice versa. To try to improve the steering a curious device was added, consisting of two heavy steel wheels hinged to the back of the chassis and pressed down on to the ground by strong springs. Steered by the driver, these tail-wheels may have made the negotiating of gentle turns simpler, but they added to the complexity of the construction, and proved in practice so vulnerable to damage that they were omitted from models after November 1916.

Going into action in a Mark 1 tank was, by all accounts, an unforgettable experience. From the outside the machine

The fate suffered by many tanks. This machine lies abandoned in a shell-hole near St Julien after the battle of Third Ypres in 1917.

looked huge, but the interior had little room to spare when it contained its full load of eight human beings, their six assorted guns, thousands of rounds of ammunition, the bulky six-cylinder engine, the three gearboxes, and the two petrol tanks of forty-six gallons capacity – enough fuel for a round trip of twenty-three miles.

Deafened by the noise of their guns and the roar of the 105 horsepower engine, half-suffocated by exhaust fumes and the smell of burnt cordite, nauseated by the constant pitching and tossing, tank crews needed a very special type of courage to continue to perform effectively in battle. Communication between crew members was difficult because of the noise and lack of light, and communication with the world outside, in the absence of radio, was possible only by means of carrier pigeons and semaphore flags. The temperature inside the tank quickly rose to above 100 degrees Fahrenheit (38 Celsius), and crews frequently suffered from exhaustion and heatstroke. Ever-present was the knowledge that it needed just one direct hit from an enemy shell to convert the machine into a blazing furnace.

The end of the road for a tank near Ypres in 1917.

The commonest hazard, which left the tank a sitting target if it occurred near the enemy's lines, was that of 'ditching'. This usually happened when the driver attempted to cross too wide a trench. He might succeed in getting the nose of the tank across, but the tail would then drop to the bottom of the trench, and in that attitude the machine lacked the power to pull itself out. Some unlucky tanks 'bellied' on top of concealed tree-stumps or similar obstructions, but many more simply sank gently but irretrievably into the mud, sometimes before they had had a chance to fire a shot.

Mud, in fact, accounts more than any other factor for the failure of tanks on the Western Front to come up to the expectations of their promoters. The machines had arrived on the scene too late, for by the time they went into action the ground was so churned up by continuous shelling that it could no longer support their weight, or else reduced their progress to an ineffectual crawl.

When the tanks made their début, on 15 September, 1916, at the battle of Flers-Courcelette, of forty-nine machines available only thirty-two reached their starting-lines, and fourteen of these either broke down or got stuck in the mud

A 'Whippet' of 1918. Light, fast, and mobile, this type of machine was designed to operate on comparatively good ground conditions beyond the enemy's main trench systems. It pointed the way to the future development of the tank.

soon after the battle began. Only nine – fewer than one in five – were able to carry out with any degree of success their task of clearing a path for the infantry through the enemy's wire and silencing the enemy's machine-guns.

It was argued at the time that the Mark 1 tanks should never have been used in such small numbers, or on such a shell-torn battleground. Later models, incorporating various mechanical and design improvements, met with some success in 1917. At Cambrai, where the ground was in fairly good condition because no preliminary bombardment had been carried out, the tanks – more than four hundred of them – managed to make deep penetrations of the German defences. But even at Cambrai the failings of the new machines were soon apparent. With nothing between the assaulting troops and open country but a half-completed line of trenches, the great attack petered out – largely because of the exhaustion of the tank crews, and the fact that by then nearly every machine urgently needed servicing and repair.

Not until the Allied offensives of 1918 did the tank begin to realise its full potential. The latest models were smaller, lighter, more mobile, and much more reliable. The so-called 'Whippet' tank weighed just fourteen tons, required a crew of only three, and had a top speed of eight m.p.h. and a range of eighty miles with a full petrol-tank. Designed specifically for 'open' warfare, it was not constructed for crossing wide trenches. What it did provide was a highly mobile fire-platform, with good protection for its crew. The Whippet was the forerunner of those German tanks which achieved such spectacular successes in Poland, France, and Russia in 1939 and 1940. One can only speculate on what the outcome might have been had Britain possessed a few hundred such machines on 1 July, 1916.

CHAPTER 11

Air Reconnaissance

> I hope none of you gentlemen is so foolish as to think that aeroplanes will be usefully employed for reconnaissance in the air. There is only one way for a commander to get information by reconnaissance and that is by the use of cavalry.

With these words the Commander-in-Chief, Aldershot, addressed some officers in 1914. One month later the Great War began, and air reconnaissance from the outset proved indispensable, while the rôle of cavalry rapidly diminished to the point of virtual extinction.

As his detractors hasten to point out, the speaker was none other than Sir Douglas Haig. On this occasion his opinion was particularly perverse. Only two years earlier, during the 1912 Army manoeuvres in East Anglia, he and General Grierson had been opposing commanders in a mock battle. Grierson's force had been allotted the use of a small airship, the *Gamma*, which had a radio transmitter capable of sending signals more than fifty miles. It proved highly successful, as the Official Historian relates:

> Every morning the *Gamma* went out at daybreak and scouted over the enemy; within half an hour the general in command was in receipt of very full information which enabled him to make out his dispositions and movements for the day. Some attempts were made to conceal troops at the halt from the view of aircraft; but, as General Grierson remarks, for troops on the move there is only one certain cover – the shades of night. So complete was the information supplied from the air that the commander of the defending force was enabled to organize his attack and end the manoeuvres a day sooner than was expected.

The Army's airship *Gamma,* which on manoeuvres in 1912 demonstrated the value of both air reconnaissance and wireless transmission. She was dismantled shortly before the outbreak of the War, having been superseded by the aeroplane.

Even before hostilities began in Europe, Grierson was making the bold claim that aircraft had 'revolutionized the art of war'; words which may have reminded some of his listeners of Wellington's celebrated maxim: *The whole art of war lies in finding out what is happening on the other side of the hill.* Soon, and under real battle conditions, it was obvious that air reconnaissance could achieve precisely that.

In the very first weeks, when the War was still one of continual rapid movement, the information supplied by the crews of the Royal Flying Corps' primitive early machines proved invaluable. They made their first operational flight on 19 August: Captain Joubert de la Ferté of No. 3 Squadron in a Blériot, Lieutenant Mapplebeck of No. 4 Squadron in a B.E. 'The machines,' as the *Official History* uncompromisingly puts it, 'lost their way and lost each other.' Nevertheless both pilots eventually landed safely and their reports, though containing little of positive significance,

A Bleriot X1 with a 35 h.p. Ansani engine. Despite their flimsy construction, such reconnaissance machines were able to furnish valuable information regarding German troop movements in the first weeks of the War.

at least indicated how easy it was to spot even small bodies of troops from the air.

Within a week of that first flight came dramatic confirmation of Grierson's prophecy. A movement by von Kluck's First Army to outflank the B.E.F. was observed from the air just in time to allow the sorely pressed British to slip away. And some days later one of the most strategically important events of the War, the change in direction of von Kluck's advance from westward to east of Paris, was confirmed by a French airman, Captain Lepic, on a reconnaissance flight from the capital. Throughout the ensuing Battle of the Marne, and the 'Race to the Sea', aerial reconnaissance played an increasing part as both sides gained in experience.

Once movement ceased and the front line congealed into a system of trenches extending from the Channel to the Alps, with the fire-swept desolation of No-Man's-Land forming an almost impenetrable barrier, then the aeroplane showed its unique capabilities.

The infantryman, peering over the parapet of his trench with a primitive periscope, might see ahead for fifty or a hundred yards, or even in places as far as the enemy's trench, but rarely farther. Everywhere his view was restricted by the wire entanglements and pickets, by shell-craters, by smashed tree-stumps and the debris of shattered buildings. All that lay beyond the enemy's wire was as hidden and mysterious as the far side of the moon.

Gun-crews, even more than infantrymen, might go for months without a glimpse of the enemy. Guns were sited wherever possible on backward-facing slopes, which gave them protection against shelling and concealed the gun-flashes to some extent from enemy observation. In their accounts, gunners stressed how rarely the order was given to 'fire over open sights' – that is, with a target actually within view. Such a situation would arise only in the course of an enemy attack, and almost always meant that the attackers had broken through the infantry defences and were alarmingly close. But more often than not, targets were first identified from the air, then photographed by aircraft cameramen, before the guns were brought into action, the fall of their shells being thereafter directed by aerial 'spotters'.

Both balloons and aeroplanes were used in spotting. Man-carrying balloons were used by the British Army as early as 1878, and were on active service in the Sudan in 1885 and in South Africa at the turn of the century. From May 1915 onwards they were used on the Western Front in increasing numbers, and became one of the most familiar features of the Somme landscape. They were naturally a favourite target for hostile aircraft firing incendiary bullets: the balloon crew, with their hydrogen-filled gasbag a mass of flames, would attempt to parachute to safety, providing those on the ground and in the trenches with a spectacle not easily forgotten.

Such balloons were of course tethered. They had some

An observation balloon near Fricourt. The winch is mounted on the vehicle to the right of the picture. Such balloons, which were filled with hydrogen, fell easy prey to enemy aircraft firing incendiary bullets.

advantages over aircraft in that they provided their crews with a relatively stable observation platform and a direct telephone link with the ground. But they lacked the versatility of powered aircraft, which as the War progressed were used more and more for bombing, trench-strafing, and air combat in addition to their main task of gathering information.

Reconnaissance was both tactical and strategical. At 3000 feet, on a clear day, an observer had a radius of vision of sixty miles, and from 20,000 feet – an altitude which by 1917 some machines could reach in ten minutes – he could see the Alps, two hundred miles to the south, as well as shipping in the Channel to his north. Usually, however, his attention would be concentrated on the position of trenches and gun batteries, and on the amount and nature of military traffic on roads and railways. Large numbers of troops could remain invisible from the air if they stayed in the shelter of woods, but as soon as they went on to roads their moving shadows betrayed them. Observers soon learned to pay special attention to rail-heads, where the quantity of rolling-stock visible could reveal much about the enemy's nocturnal activities: an increase overnight suggested that reinforcements had been brought up during the hours of darkness, while an increase during the day pointed to a possible withdrawal after nightfall.

Despite great improvements in the art of camouflage, some activities, notes the Official Historian, defied concealment:

> The construction of new roads or railway sidings, the pushing forward of railheads, the building of hutments in other areas, the establishment of dumps or new aerodromes, are all material for knowledge of the enemy's intentions . . .

'Spotting' – that is, reporting on the fall of shells on enemy positions to ensure accuracy of range and direction – was to remain a vital function of the new arm throughout the War. It is strange to recall that at first no proper system existed of map reference. To identify a target on the map it was described as being, for example, 'slightly north of the letter '*h*' in '*Cuinchy*''. This was too clumsy, time-consuming, and inexact for Lieutenant D.S. Lewis, a pioneer in the development of air-to-ground communication. In September 1914 he drew identical squared grids on maps prepared for himself and the commander of the artillery battery, so that by quoting two coordinates any spot on the map or on the ground could be instantly pinpointed. Such maps were soon made available for the entire Western Front. Lewis's system of grid reference remains in use everywhere to this day.

Lewis's next invention was the clock-code ranging disc. In its final version this took the form of a transparent circular disc, on which were painted the figures of a clock-face and concentric circles of radii equivalent to 10, 25, 50, and 100 yards on the map, each circle bearing an identifying letter. The disc was pinned to the map with its centre on the target and the 12 o'clock-6 o'clock line running north-south. The clock figures gave the direction, and the circles the distance,

The War provided a great stimulus to the development of aircraft design. This quite sophisticated-looking B.E.2 is of a type much in demand during the battles of the Somme for artillery 'spotting'.

of each shellburst from the target, as noted by the air-spotter. He then passed this information to the battery commander, who made the necessary corrections to his guns. Great accuracy could be rapidly achieved, with consequent saving of valuable ammunition.

These devices would have been of little value in the absence of efficient means of communication. The first wireless sets used in aircraft weighed some 75lb. (34 kg.) and were so bulky they took up all the space usually occupied by an observer, as well as encroaching on what had been allotted to the pilot. But in the autumn of 1915 a compact set was produced which weighed less than 20 lb. (9 kg.) and had the additional advantage of leaving room for an observer.

By the summer of 1916 and the start of the Battle of the Somme, British fighter pilots had gained an ascendancy over their German counterparts, mainly by developing the French practice of 'offensive patrolling', in which formations of fighter aircraft deliberately sought out the enemy and engaged him in combat before he could approach the more vulnerable reconnaissance machines. This gave the British reconnaissance aircraft freedom to concentrate on their task of gathering information, which by that time included photographing in detail the entire German front as well as a wide tract of country behind.

Aerial photographs had been taken by British airmen during the Battle of the Aisne (September 1914), but the results on that occasion were blurred and unimpressive. Both in apparatus and technique the British lagged behind their French allies, but with their help a small but efficient Photographic Section was functioning in each corps squadron, as well as in each army reconnaissance squadron, before the opening of the Somme offensive.

On 1 July the Flying Corps mustered 185 aircraft in the area of the Somme. Their duties were wide-ranging, and included counter-battery spotting, the destruction of enemy balloons, and the bombing of all enemy railways which could be used to bring up reserve troops, as well as close reconnaissance of the battlefield itself. The extent of the advance, revealed by sunlight glinting on the mirrors which the troops carried, was noted by the airmen on their maps; and various coded signals were devised so that the troops on the ground could pass information to aircraft, and thence back to their divisional headquarters. In the event, only two of these coded signals were needed in the sector opposite Beaumont Hamel: '*XX*', meaning '*Held up by machine-gun fire*', and '*ZZ*', meaning '*Held up by barbed wire*'.

During and after the War, popular attention focused, understandably, on the activities of the Corps' fighter pilots, whose death-or-glory duels above the trenches could hardly fail to capture the imagination. But here we have remembered that the Corps was born of the need to discover what lay 'on the other side of the hill', and that reconnaissance remained its principal function throughout the War.

CHAPTER 12

Beaumont Hamel: the first British assault

Military disasters hold for the British an appeal which no
military success can hope to match. Thus the events of 1
July, 1916 still claim attention, not only from military
historians and commentators, but from playwrights, feature
writers, broadcasters and television journalists; whereas the
final battle of the Somme seldom receives even a passing
mention.

The earlier battle was a tragic failure, the later a brilliant
success. The assault on 1 July was launched along a much
wider front; and we can best compare the two occasions if we
confine our attention to that portion of the front which they
had in common, the sector opposite the miniature fortress of
Beamont Hamel.

When the Somme offensive opened, the German line at
Beaumont Hamel still ran where it had been established after
the 'Race to the Sea' in 1914; but in the interval no effort had
been spared to strengthen its defences. After an attack in
November, 1914 by French troops – an attack which
foundered against uncut wire – Beaumont Hamel had been
rendered seemingly impregnable.

The site possessed great defensive advantages. The village
itself, which once consisted of some 160 houses grouped
round a picturesque white church, had long since been
reduced by shellfire to rubble; but amid the ruins were deep
cellars which the Germans had converted into secure
dug-outs, with the entrances facing away from the British
artillery, and protected by barbed-wire entanglements on an
unprecedented scale. Below the village ruins, and radiating
outwards, a labyrinth of tunnels had been constructed, in
which whole companies of men could shelter during a
bombardment, and through which they could move safely
and rapidly to counter an attack.

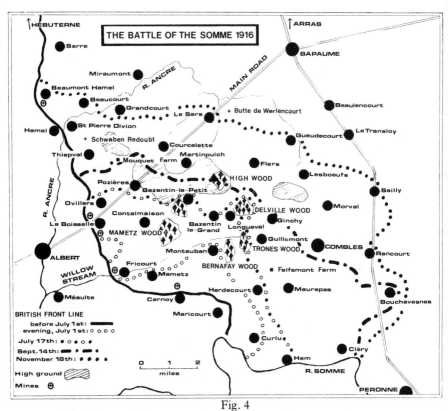

Fig. 4

Three and a half centuries earlier, at the time of the Wars of Religion, rudimentary tunnels had been dug out of the chalk as places of refuge for the villagers. These tunnels the Germans had greatly enlarged and extended, shoring up the entrances with stout timbers, installing electric light, and bringing in articles of furniture to provide comfortable quarters for their officers. In some tunnels they had even set up well-stocked tailors' and jewellers' shops.

Above ground, every care had been taken to ensure that all terrain over which an attack might come was under observation and accessible to defensive fire. Running from east to west a quarter of a mile south of the village lay the sinister-sounding Y-Ravine, a natural gully 800 yards long and 30 feet deep: its steep sides were now riddled with

Zero hour on 1 July, 1916, was 7.30 a.m. Here, as the sun climbs and the sky lightens, men in the British trenches facing Beaumont Hamel rouse their sleeping companions and prepare for the assault.

concealed dug-outs leading back to the underground passages.

The British, for their part, could hardly have been in a less favourable position from which to launch an attack. The Official Historian described the site thus:

The battle-ground formed a kind of amphitheatre: the VIII Corps seemed confronted with tiers of fire and was under complete observation by the enemy, so that even its field artillery suffered from the German counter-batteries, as, though well dug in, the flashes of the guns were visible. Its own position, sloping to the front, gave it no more than command of the German front line and support trenches; observation – and most of the artillery observers had to be near the front line – was limited by the ridges beyond; there were thus many places close to the front on which ground observation was impossible. Moreover, the convex shape of the slope on the British side made it difficult to bring heavy gun fire on the enemy front position, and there were therefore parts of it which were hardly touched by the preliminary bombardment.

Why, with such obvious disadvantages facing it, was the attack allowed to go ahead?

Two considerations helped to bolster confidence: a carefully calculated 'creeping' barrage had been planned; and a huge mine was to be blown just before the assault began.

As regards the barrage, the instructions from Corps Headquarters were that whereas the heavy artillery would make only six 'lifts' – increases in range – between the German front line and the third objective, 4000 yards distant, the divisional field artillery would 'assist the infantry by lifting very slowly 50 yards each minute, i.e., at the same rate as it is calculated the infantry will advance'. Ominously, the instructions added:

> The times once settled cannot be altered. The infantry must therefore make their pace conform to the rate of the artillery lifts. If the infantry find themselves checked by our barrage, they must halt and wait till the barrage moves forward.

Thus this first attempt at what came to be known as a 'creeping' barrage was confined to field artillery firing 18-pounder shrapnel, and would not even begin to take effect until the infantry had crossed No-Man's-Land – which south of Beaumont Hamel was as much as 500 yards wide in places. At the 'calculated walking rate' of fifty yards per minute this

7.45 a.m. on 1 July, 1916, at Beaumont Hamel. The white debris from the newly-blown mine can be made out on the right of the picture. Men of the 29th Division are retiring before a hail of machine-gun bullets coming from the crater and from beyond Hawthorn Ridge. Casualties in the 29th Division were enormous, and not one yard of ground was gained by nightfall.

meant that the slowly advancing waves of infantry would be without artillery protection for the whole of that critical period of ten minutes which would follow the ending of the preliminary bombardment and the beginning of the assault.

A similar small but equally momentous instance of mis-timing was to involve the Hawthorn Redoubt mine. A quarter of a mile west of Beaumont Hamel, where Hawthorn Ridge overlooked the village, a mine had been laid beneath the German strongpoint which dominated the valley. Into it had been packed 40,000 pounds of ammonal. After some debate, a decision was made to blow this mine at Zero minus ten minutes. Simultaneously with the blowing of the mine, the field howitzers firing on the forward enemy machine-gun emplacements in that sector would lift to allow the mine crater to be occupied. But through a series of misunderstandings, or from sheer error of judgement, an order was in fact given for the field howitzers *of the entire Corps* to lift simultaneously at Zero minus ten. This mistake was to have the most tragic consequences for the advancing infantrymen.

Other preparations had included the excavation of approach tunnels from the British lines to within a few yards of the enemy trenches. Two of these were opened in front of Beaumont Hamel at 2 a.m. on 1 July, and Stokes mortars installed in them. Elsewhere, lanes had been cut through the British wire, and bridges laid across rear trenches to make it easy for large numbers of troops to move forward rapidly. But above all, reliance was being placed on the effectiveness of the preliminary bombardment, which began all along the eighteen mile front on 24 June.

An ambitious artillery programme had been drawn up. The main purpose of the bombardment was to cut the enemy wire, but in addition every aspect of the enemy's defences was brought under fire: trenches, approach roads, rail-heads, sidings, ammunition dumps, billets, observation posts, woods that might be sheltering troops, and every village and building that was within range of the guns. General Rawlinson, whose Fourth Army was to make the attack, could muster one field gun per twenty-one yards and one heavy gun per fifty-seven yards, which during the whole bombardment fired a total of 1,700,000 rounds. Impressive figures; but in fact many of the guns were obsolete and inaccurate in aim, and much ammunition was to prove defective, either failing altogether to explode or bursting prematurely. Moreover the programme, designed for a bombardment lasting five days, had to be expanded because of bad weather to last a week. For that particular setback Rawlinson can hardly be blamed; but he was certainly culpable in failing to obtain confirmation of the effectiveness of the bombardment before launching his attack. In far too many sectors, and particularly at Beaumont Hamel, it was discovered too late that the enemy wire had survived intact,

Flame throwers, introduced by the Germans in 1915, were first used by the British on 1 July, 1916. Oil under pressure was ignited by a jet and hosed across No-Man's-Land, with the terrifying result shown above. Flame throwers were effective only where the trenches were very close, since the maximum range of the hoses was fifty yards.

and that some German trenches were even quite unscathed.

The VIII Corps, which was to carry out the assault in the Beaumont Hamel sector, was commanded by Lieutenant-General Sir A.G. Hunter-Weston. Directly facing the village was the division which he had commanded at Gallipoli, where it had earned for itself the sobriquet 'the Incomparable 29th'. It had not yet seen action in France. On its left was the 4th Division, composed like the 29th of Regulars, and beyond them was a 'New Army' division, the 31st.

The intense bombardment of the previous week had of course alerted the Germans to the coming attack. The explosion of the Hawthorn Redoubt mine at Zero minus ten minutes gave them more than enough time to scramble up the steps from the safety of their dug-outs and take up effective firing positions – particularly since, as mentioned earlier, the barrage on their forward positions had lifted by then. Even before the waves of infantry started to move forward, German machine-guns and rifles were spraying No-Man's-Land with bullets, while a fierce barrage began to fall on the congested British trenches. It came from sixty-six German batteries which had survived the British bombardment: many had not even been identified before they began firing. For this and other examples of faulty intelligence Hunter-Weston's men were doomed to pay a heavy price.

Those who survived to climb out of their trenches and make the perilous journey across No-Man's-Land found themselves facing inadequately cut wire and machine-guns firing at point-blank range. Even the mine on Hawthorn Ridge failed in its purpose: when two platoons of Royal Fusiliers rushed towards it they found the farther lip of the immense crater already occupied by enemy machine-guns.

Farther south, too, all was disaster. The wire entanglement along the rim of Y-Ravine was discovered to have been untouched by the bombardment, and as they struggled to penetrate it the attackers were caught by machine-gun fire coming from the many concealed dug-outs in the walls of the ravine. There the South Wales Borderers lost 372 officers and men; and that battalion's losses proved to be among the *lowest* in the whole Division.

An hour and a half after Zero, the 1st Essex and the Newfoundland Regiment were ordered forward. The Essex at first found themselves physically unable to move because of the crush of heaped-up bodies of dead and dying in their trench. The Newfoundlanders were left to approach Y-Ravine on their own, and some even reached the German wire; 710 became casualties within a space of minutes, including every single officer except the C.O. and the Adjutant.

All along the front of VIII Corps the picture was the same. When darkness fell on 1 July, with here and there some futile attacks still continuing, the front line in the sector as a whole was exactly where it had been at Zero hour.

The VIII Corps suffered more than 14,000 casualties that day – the highest total for any Corps taking part in the offensive. In its vain assault on Beaumont Hamel the 29th Division lost 223 officers and 5017 other ranks.

The enemy facing them, the 119th Reserve Regiment, lost 8 officers killed and 3 wounded, 93 other ranks killed and 188 wounded: a total of 292.

CHAPTER 13

The second British assault

(1)

After 1 July the British offensive on the Somme became in effect a step-by-step siege operation against the German position. Here and there a few hundred yards of ground were gained, but the cost in men and materials was immense. The last real hope of breaking right through the lines of defence and out into open country vanished with the disappointing performance of the tanks on 15 September. Of the five cavalry divisions which would have effected that break-out – the force which had inspired such naive faith at the start of the battle – three were sent down the line the following day and by implication consigned to oblivion; two token divisions were allowed to remain, but even the most sanguine cavalryman must has guessed that his day was already over.

In some important ways the offensive had not been without results. Its immediate aim, to divert German pressure from Verdun, had been achieved: during August, in fact, the initiative there had passed to the French, and the Germans acknowledged their failure by banishing their Chief of Staff to the newly-formed Rumanian front – where he soon redeemed his reputation. Hindenburg took over from Falkenhayn on 28 August, with Ludendorff as his able Quartermaster-General.

A secondary aim of the offensive – to wear down German resistance – was beginning to show definite signs of success. Intelligence reports, especially those compiled from the interrogation of prisoners, revealed a distinct deterioration in the enemy's morale. No similar weakening was to be found on the British side, despite a comparable, and in places a considerably higher, rate of casualties. What the enemy was finding particularly disheartening, it appeared, were certain

A helping hand for a Highlander from a Scots Guardsman. It is autumn 1916. Here on the Somme the mud was more deadly, in the opinion of those who came to know both areas, than at Passchendaele in 1917.

unequivocal signs of the superior material resources upon which the British could draw; should the war continue long enough, these resources would be bound to affect the outcome.

Less important than the immediate or the secondary aim, but still desirable, was the seizure of the high ground, of the strongpoints in woods, and of certain tactically advantageous locations in the region between the Somme and its tributary the Ancre. By the end of October almost all such positions had fallen into British hands; with one important exception. North of the river Ancre, and almost hidden between spurs of hills running down to the river, Beaumont Hamel still posed a grave threat to Haig's forces. Possession of the fortress would not only lessen, during the coming winter, the risks and discomforts of the British troops now occupying the northern slopes of the ridge between the Ancre and the Somme, but it would also provide them with a far better jumping-off base when the offensive was renewed – as Haig fully intended it should be – in the Spring.

Preparations for another attack had begun early in October, when a fresh mine shaft was dug towards Hawthorn Crater, and the Russian saps used on 1 July were overhauled and strengthened. On 21 October an important advance was made south of the Ancre, on a front of 7000 yards, securing all the high ground overlooking the river. Now at last the Ancre valley could be kept under direct observation, and the artillery proceeded to make good use of their new opportunities. General Gough, commanding the Reserve Army – renamed the Fifth Army on 30 October – had one heavy gun for every 31 yards of front, and one field gun or howitzer to every 13.5 yards: a considerable increase on the corresponding figures of 57 yards and 21 yards for 1 July. When the German commanders realised that Beaumont Hamel was becoming a target for guns firing from north, west, and south, evacuation of the area was seriously discussed. But General von Below, commanding the German First Army, was most unwilling to relinquish the advantages of the high ground north of the Ancre valley, and in any case he was convinced that the positions at Serre and Beaumont Hamel could withstand any assault which the British were capable of delivering.

His greatest ally, and one which against a lesser opponent might have proved decisive, was the weather, which since mid-September had been atrocious. In October the whole countryside was reported to be 'awash'. The Official Historian, who usually minimises rather than exaggerates difficulties, admits that conditions were now so bad as to make mere existence a trial of body and spirit:

> Little could be seen from the air through the rain and mist, so counter-battery work suffered and it was often impossible to locate with any accuracy the new German trenches and shell-hole positions . . . Bursts of high explosive were smothered in the ooze . . .; in some partially flooded battery positions sinking platforms had to be restored with any battle debris that came to hand. The ground was so deep in mud that to

E

The Somme, 1916. Two mules are being engulfed by mud in a shell-hole. Spectators are powerless to help: if they attempt to do so, they themselves will get sucked into the quagmire.

move one 18-pdr. ten or twelve horses were often needed, and, to supplement the supplies brought up by light-railway and pack-horse, ammunition had to be dragged up on sledges improvised of sheets of corrugated iron. The infantry, sometimes wet to the skin and almost exhausted before zero hour, were often condemned to struggle painfully forward through the mud under heavy fire against objectives vaguely defined and difficult of recognition.

The battleground of Passchendaele in Flanders is often mentioned as the one where mud was at its worst, but the slippery, chalky mud of the Ancre valley was, in the opinion of men familiar with both, even more dangerous and depressing. In communication trenches the mud was sometimes waist-high, and a relieving battalion might take up to three hours to reach its destination three miles away – to the disgust of those waiting to be relieved. No man could now travel alone in safety, for 'the mud took on an aggressive, wolf-like guise, and like a wolf could pull down

Waggons laden with fodder for horses pull to the side of the road to let the big guns, drawn by Holt caterpillar tractors, move up to Beaumont Hamel, Autumn 1916.

and swallow the lonely wanderer in the darkness.'

Conditions above ground on the German side of the wire were of course no better, and the defenders there unwisely began to take the view that the weather had put a stop to further British assaults. In their deep, better drained, well-ventilated, and comparatively warm dug-outs beneath the rubble of Beaumont Hamel they prepared to stick it out passively through the approaching winter.

And for the British, time was running out. A month had passed since individual battalions had begun practising their attacks, originally planned for 12 October. Repeated postponements strained everyone's nerves, but commanders at all levels knew that until conditions on the ground improved there would be little chance of success. The heavy rain had not merely filled every trench with mud; it impeded the forward movement of the guns, held up supply wagons, brought tanks to a standstill, cut down visibility for the gunners and their spotters, and greatly hampered the activities of the Flying Corps, especially the machines engaged on photographic reconnaissance.

In the first week of November the rain diminished, but the weather remained so unsettled that most brigade and battalion commanders thought the attack should be cancelled. On them fell the responsibility for maintaining morale, and understandably they were beginning to wonder how much longer that elusive quality could be kept at fighting pitch.

Then, on 9 November, the rain at last stopped. The thermometer started to fall: the waterlogged ground hardened, froze, and soon vehicles could move without immediately sinking up to their axle-shafts. In bright, clear skies the squadrons of the Flying Corps began once again to quarter the enemy's trench system.

General Gough, having conferred at length with his subordinate commanders, reached a difficult and courageous decision: his attack would go forward on Monday, 13 November; Zero hour to be at 5.45 a.m., one and a half hours before dawn.

(2)

From the north to south, seven divisions would take part. The 51st (Highland) Division, directly opposite Beaumont Hamel, was flanked on its left by the 2nd, 3rd and 31st Divisions, and on its right by the 63rd, 39th, and 19th Divisions. Experience had shown that in assaults along frontages of any length, successful penetration was likely to be deepest at the centre and least towards the flanks. The 51st Division, at the very middle of the five-mile-long front to be attacked, was thus in a favoured position; but the task it faced was from every point of view formidable.

The German 'front line' in fact consisted of three, and in some places four, lines of trenches, more or less parallel to each other, and inter-connected by many communication trenches – one every fifty or a hundred yards – running from

General Sir Hubert Gough, whose offensive on the Ancre culminated in the capture of Beaumont Hamel. After that battle his reputation stood high; but in 1918, following the initial successes of the Germans' Spring offensive, he was relieved of his Command – a political decision which he accepted without rancour. Military historians now agree that in 1918 Gough and his 5th Army were given an almost impossible task.

front to rear. Each of those lines had its own protective screen of barbed wire, and no matter how thorough the initial bombardment, some wire entanglements were bound to escape destruction.

South of the village, as described in the previous chapter, lay Y-Ravine, menacing any direct approach from that quarter, while to the west the crater left by the Hawthorn Ridge mine on 1 July had been strongly fortified and now bristled with enemy machine-gun posts.

The British policy of continual harassment and frequent small raids, persisted in throughout the summer, had resulted in the Germans redoubling their defensive precautions. Numerous new strongholds had been constructed at key points in the labyrinth of trenches. The walls of the trenches themselves were buttressed, dug-outs deepened and strengthened so as to withstand shellfire better, and dug-out entrances – some had as many as seven – were shored up with strong timbers and iron rails. Elsewhere on the Somme, as we now know, the Germans had already begun work on plans for a stategic withdrawal, but evidently they had no intention yet of quitting the fortress of Beaumont Hamel.

Gough for his part, though by temperament an optimist, showed from the start that he harboured no illusions regarding the difficulty of his task. His first act was to add weight to his artillery by borrowing twelve siege batteries, plus the artillery of three divisions, from his northern neighbour, the Third Army. Over a shorter frontage he was thus able to deliver a heavier bombardment than had been put down by the Fourth Army artillery on 1 July; nor was it, as then, a uniform barrage, but one which concentrated its fire on specifically selected targets. Moreover, every morning from the end of October, an intense barrage was dropped on the frontline German trenches during the hour before sunrise, in the hope that when the actual assault came, its opening bombardment might be mistaken by the defenders for part of an established routine.

One weapon was particularly suited to the positions about to be assaulted, and Gough made full use of it. The warren of dug-outs in Y-Ravine and the catacombs beneath Beaumont Hamel might resist high explosives, but nothing could prevent poison gas from silently filtering down into their recesses, causing havoc among unsuspecting or dilatory

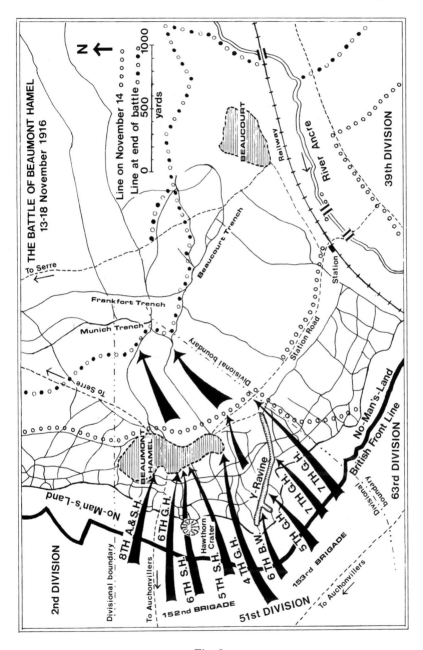

Fig. 5

occupants. On 28 October an intensive gas bombardment was delivered against both targets, starting with a disabling lachrymatory gas and following up with the deadly 'White Star' mixture of chlorine and phosgene. On this occasion the Special Brigade for the first time used 40-pound gas-bombs fired from 9.5-inch mortars. Such bombs were appropriately nick-named '*Judgements*', and their inventor calculated that, employed in sufficient numbers, they could reduce the cost of killing Germans to a modest 16 shillings (80p) per head. Two days before the big attack, another heavy gas bombardment was delivered against both Y-Ravine and the village itself.

As dusk fell on Sunday, 12 November, 44,000 infantrymen – more in number than all the British at Waterloo or on the D-Day Normandy beaches – began moving forwards to their assembly-points. Everywhere they found the communication trenches waterlogged. The 51st Division's 153rd Brigade took four hours to cover two and a half miles: their assembly trenches turned out to be uninhabitable, so they spent the rest of that bitterly cold night lying in the open behind the parados. Their compatriots in the 152nd Brigade, with twice as far to march, sensibly halted halfway for food and mugs of tea. They managed to reach their destination with an hour to spare before Zero.

And now Nature, which till then had seemed so hostile, capriciously decided to favour the attackers. As the night wore on, a bank of raw fog stole up from the valley of the Ancre, obscuring the pale crescent of the westering moon, blotting out the flickering gun-flashes, and shrouding the troops still groping their way to their assembly-points. Recognising a rare opportunity, parties of the 7th Gordon Highlanders crept out into No-Man's-Land at Zero minus ten minutes, taking whatever cover was available while the 'routine' pre-dawn bombardment, which the Germans had now come to expect, poured down ahead of them. At 5.45 a.m. precisely, the real barrage opened, the new Hawthorn Crater mine erupted, and all along the 8000-yard front the

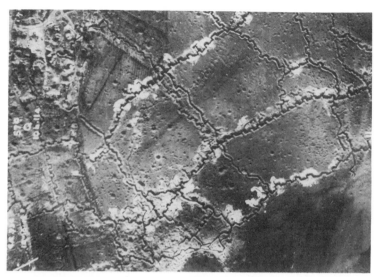

Part of the German trench-system at Beaumont Hamel. The village is in the left upper corner. The dark semi-circle halfway along the bottom margin of the photograph is Hawthorn Crater. No-Man's-Land is in the right lower corner, and Y-Ravine is just beyond the right-hand edge of this aerial photograph.

infantry moved forward to the attack.

Hugging the barrage as closely as they dared, two companies of the 7th Gordons – they formed the extreme right wing of the 51st Division – reached the enemy wire to find it well cut and readily negotiable. Here the defenders, dazed by the intensity of the barrage and the speed of the assault, could offer but little resistance to the kilted figures looming suddenly out of the fog. Once the barrage moved on, at a rate of a hundred yards every five minutes, the Highlanders had no difficulty in taking line after line of trenches south of Y-Ravine. They arrived at their first objective, the road from Beaumont Hamel to its railway station near the Ancre, at 6.45 a.m., exactly on time.

Y-Ravine itself, as expected, proved to be the most formidable obstacle facing the Division that day. A hurricane barrage had been directed into its depths at Zero hour, but as men of the 6th Black Watch and 7th Gordons approached it

Mud at Beaumont Hamel, November 1916. The man on the left has just been pulled from mud into which he had sunk up to his armpits. Many were less fortunate.

they were met with a storm of fire from concealed machine-guns and rifles. Tanks, no doubt, could have dealt easily with such a problem, but the two machines allotted to the Division had as yet failed to negotiate the mud. Dogged fighting was the only solution, and time was not on the side of the Highlanders. It was now daylight, and although the dense fog persisted, continuing to obscure the frantic German rocket-signals to their artillery, the vital element of surprise had gone.

As the morning wore on, the 5th Gordons, drawn in from Support, were committed to desperate hand-to-hand fighting in and around the Ravine, while the 7th Black Watch toiled through the mud to keep them supplied with grenades and ammunition. At one stage more than a hundred men were pinned down in Y-Ravine by enemy fire from every quarter. The situation was one demanding the utmost in individual enterprise, since by 10 a.m. almost all the runners had been killed or wounded, and for a while all communication links

Beaumont Hamel soon after its capture. Behind the group of men is all that remains of the village church. Every house in the village had been damaged beyond recognition by the British bombardments, but under these ruins were tunnels and caves which had sheltered whole battalions of defenders.

with Battalion Headquarters were broken. Nearly five hours of continuous bloody conflict were required before resistance in Y-Ravine began to crumble; by then its western salient had been turned, and the 6th Black Watch and 4th Gordons were moving into the outskirts of the village. The 5th Gordons, having taken more than 300 prisoners, re-established communications by setting up their Battalion Headquarters in one of the captured strongholds in Y-Ravine.

Meanwhile the advance on the northern half of the village was proceeding well. The mine beneath Hawthorn Crater, charged with no less than thirteen tons of ammonal, had exploded with appalling violence exactly on Zero hour, obliterating at least six German dug-outs and entombing more than three hundred of their occupants. Within seconds

Splintered trunks show where a wood once stood. This photograph was taken near Beaumont Hamel in November 1916.

the new crater, still hot and smouldering, was swarming with 5th Seaforth Highlanders: the defenders had lost a most vital strongpoint. Farther north, however, men of the 5th Seaforths and of the 8th Argyll & Sutherland Highlanders, encountering a veritable sea of mud in their particular sector of No-Man's-Land, dropped too far behind the creeping barrage and were caught by machine-guns firing from the German second and third trench lines. Both the support battalion (6th Seaforths) and the reserves (6th Gordons) were brought forward to deal with this hold-up. In the ensuing grenade duel the techniques of the Highlanders' well-trained bombing squads proved superior, and the offending machine-guns were effectively subdued.

Now, with Hawthorn Crater and Y-Ravine both disposed of, it remained only to storm the village itself. The claws of the beast had been removed; what was now needed was to sever its spinal cord.

By a stroke of luck a map had been captured which revealed the exact positions of two enemy battalion headquarters. One platoon of the 8th Argylls, led by Lieut. W.D.Munro, and another of the 6th Seaforths, led by Lieut. G.V. Edwards, headed straight for these nerve centres, and soon had the satisfaction of making both headquarters staffs their prisoners. (Neither of these young officers was to survive the War).

Thereafter, such resistance as remained within the fortress inevitably began to disintegrate, but it was not until darkness had covered the battlefield that the last cellar was cleared and the last cave and dug-out rendered harmless. Meanwhile, an advance by the Division beyond the eastern edge of the village to Frankfort Trench, the second objective of the day, could easily have been effected. However, no contact could be made on the right with the 63rd Division's 188th Brigade, which on reaching its second objective could find no way of communicating that news to the rear. Wisely, the 5th Gordons arranged to form a defensive flank running back to the former German front line.

On the 51st Division's left, where the 2nd Division was attacking Redan ridge, a battalion of the Highland Light Infantry made rapid progress north of the village, but units which advanced further were obliged to withdraw to the lane running north from Beaumont Hamel to Serre. Here they made contact with their countrymen of the 51st Division, and a secure line was established.

Reviewing the whole of his front at the end of the day, General Gough could be well satisfied. South of the Ancre, the 39th Division had done splendidly, taking many prisoners at comparatively little cost, and the front there had been pushed forward as much as 2000 yards in places. North of the river, the 63rd Division had reached its first objective and was poised to take Beaucourt. The 51st Division had of course been spectacularly successful in storming Beaumont Hamel, the day's major prize. Some progress had been made by the 2nd Division; but the two most northerly divisions, the 3rd and the 31st, were unable to hold on to what little ground they had gained – at a fearful price – and were now

The battlefield of Beaumont Hamel, photographed two weeks after the attack. Y-Ravine, where the fighting was fiercest, runs diagonally in the middle distance.

back in their starting-off trenches. Serre, one of the objectives for 1 July, remained as firmly as ever in enemy hands.

At dawn the next day the assault was renewed. A few minor gains were made in the south, but no significant advances elsewhere. The 63rd Division, meeting but feeble resistance, took Beaucourt village and some trenches beyond, before being relieved. The 51st Division, which by then had been in the line for six successive weeks, had to wait three more days before the order for its relief came through. Its attacks on 14 November were bedevilled by communication problems, and it had to endure that most discouraging of mishaps – being shelled out of a newly captured trench by its own artillery.

Nevertheless, the 51st Division was in high spirits when it finally went back down the line on 17 November. It had achieved a notable feat of arms in the most adverse of circumstances. More than 2000 prisoners were officially credited to the Division, though at the height of the fighting

An officer of the 51st Division counts German prisoners as they come in during the battle of Beaumont Hamel. The Division's final score exceeded 2000.

many more had been handed over to the safekeeping of less heavily involved units.

And there had been spoils of war in abundance, for the tunnels and caves under Beaumont Hamel had yielded huge stores of military booty – rifles, machine-guns, mortars, mortar-bombs, grenades, small-arms ammunition, and even a complete armourer's shop – as well as items of much more immediate interest to the troops, such as brown bread, tins of Argentinian corned beef, Norwegian sardines, bacon, and dried fruits, not to mention luxuries like wines and cigars.

Someone, so legend has it, even managed to discover beneath the rubble a usable piano.

CHAPTER 14

Conclusions

Some of the reasons for the 51st Division's success on 13 November are not hard to identify. The fog which blanketed the battlefield, although it caused the advancing infantry to lose direction in places, was in general much more damaging to the defenders. In battle, when other means of communication failed, the German forward troops relied on their coloured flares to direct their artillery; but in the fog these S.O.S. signals went unnoticed. With visibility reduced to thirty yards, the enemy machine-gunners were not only deprived of targets but themselves fell victim more readily to grenade or sniper's bullet. Again, by heightening the confusion and alarm of those at the receiving end of the assault, the fog led to more defenders surrendering than might have been expected. Over 7000 prisoners were collected by the seven attacking divisions – more than 2000 of them by the 51st Division alone; a figure that should be compared with the total of 1983 prisoners taken by the eighteen British divisions which attacked on 1 July.

Darkness, as well as fog, cloaked the initial phase of the attack on 13 November. On 1 July Rawlinson had originally suggested a time just before sunrise for the great advance, but the French overruled him, insisting upon visual observation for their artillery bombardment. Rawlinson, however, went on to demonstrate the advantages of a night attack in his successful assaults on Bazentin-le-Petit and Bazentin-le-Grand on 14 July, and Gough was convinced, and was in due course able to prove, that his own Fifth Army troops were now sufficently trained to undertake a similar operation.

Since 1 July artillery techniques had begun to improve. Gough not only had much greater firepower at his disposal, but his gun-crews were more experienced, more familiar with their weapons, and better served by their spotters on the ground and in the air. Targets could now be located with great accuracy, thanks to advances in aerial photography, and more subtle methods of dealing with them had been evolved. With the object of isolating an area under attack and so preventing reserves from reaching it, all its roads and approach routes were bombarded, as well as the area itself; and to create further confusion, other fronts were simultaneously bombarded although no actual attacks were contemplated there. The problem of cutting the enemy wire remained intractable, but better results were obtained by Gough's field artillery than by Rawlinson's heavy guns, which had left the ground so deeply cratered as to impede the infantry's advance.

Any particularly heavy bombardment would always suggest to the defenders that an attack was imminent, and only its precise time and place remained uncertain. On 1 July the sudden lifting of the British barrage at Zero hour gave the enemy clear warning of the impending attack, and ample time to climb from their dug-outs and set up their machine-guns. As has so often been pointed out, the British lost their race to the German wire by approximately ten minutes; and 57,000 casualties resulted. By November, however, the skill of the British gunners, the accuracy of their weapons, and the reliability of their ammunition had all been increased to the point where a rudimentary form of 'creeping' barrage could be attempted, giving the infantry at least some protection during their hazardous crossing of No-Man's-Land. Not until late in the War was a really flexible artillery programme made possible, that could meet all the rapidly changing conditions of battle.

At no time during the Battles of the Somme were nearly enough gas-shells available. As far back as 16 May, Haig had asked for 40,000 rounds for the coming offensive; by the end of July, the figure he was quoting was 30,000 *weekly*. With factories in Britain quite unable to provide such huge totals

An enemy shell bursts just beyond the British wire east of Beaumont Hamel, December 1916. Snow now covers the ground.

he was obliged, for most of the battle, to rely on French batteries for his gas bombardments. At Beaumont Hamel, however, the new Livens projector was, as we have seen, used with good effect against both the village and Y-Ravine.

The *Official History* makes the curious claim that Beaumont Hamel was finally taken 'with the aid of tanks', but there is no evidence that they played any significant part in the battle. Indeed, in some respects they simply complicated matters: an attempt to move some tanks into the area on 11 November merely produced a memorable traffic-jam. During the afternoon of 13 November, when the 51st Division was already in Beaumont Hamel, two tanks were ordered forward from Auchonvillers. One came to grief in the mud immediately beyond the German wire, and the other was ditched soon after, just north of the village. (Determined not to miss out, the Scottish commander of one of these machines 'persuaded' some German prisoners to carry his tank's machine-guns up to the battle-front, where he proceeded to make himself useful in the process of consolidation.) In the somewhat better conditions on the front of the 63rd Division, one tank did assist in subduing strongpoints on 14 November; but in general the failings of the machines greatly outweighed their possible value.

When the events of 1 July and 13 November are compared, nowhere are the differences more striking than in the infantry tactics employed on the two occasions. With only slight exaggeration it could be said that 1 July looked back to Waterloo, whereas 13 November saw practices that were accepted as routine in the war of 1939-45.

Paramount on 1 July was the theory that the advance should conform to a rigid timetable, with the infantry moving slowly forward in successive lines not more than 100 yards apart, each man separated from his neighbours by an interval of two or three paces. The logic for this archaic formation was chillingly explained in a memorandum, *Training of Divisions for Offensive Action*, dated 8 May, 1916:

> A single line of men has usually failed, two lines have generally failed but sometimes succeeded, three lines have generally succeeded, but sometimes failed, and four or more lines have generally succeeded.

Sheer weight of numbers, in other words, could prove effective; and besides, what was the alternative?

> Officers and troops generally do not now possess that military knowledge arising from a long and high state of training which enables them to act promptly on sound lines in unexpected situations.

Such thinly-veiled contempt for the men of the new 'civilian' armies was soon dispelled by their performance in battle; but the policy of advancing infantry to a rigid timetable was not wholly abandoned until much later in the War, and then only with reluctance.

In Major-General G.M.Harper the 51st Division possessed an exceptionally gifted commander. His troops had already shown something of their mettle on 22 July in an attack on

Major-General Sir G.M. Harper, who commanded the Highland Division at Beaumont Hamel, attends the 7th Black Watch Sports on 10 May, 1917. Harper was a keen student of tactics, and much of the Division's success at Beaumont Hamel was due to his careful attention to tactical details, and to his insistence upon thorough preparation and training.

High Wood, but there they had been denied any opportunity of making a planned, coordinated assault, and little had been achieved, despite heavy losses. By November, however, the Division was not only battle-tested but thoroughly familiar with the particular skills demanded by the terrain. All its battalions had practised street-fighting and assaults on fortified villages, and had been taught the best ways of flushing out the enemy from the deep dug-outs and tunnels known to exist in and around Beaumont Hamel. In particular, their bombing squads were well-rehearsed in their duties: these men were to play a key rôle in the attack on Y-Ravine.

No amount of rehearsal and training, however, could foresee all the problems encountered in the real battle, and in the end it was, as always, the calibre of the officers and men themselves that decided the outcome. The unusual weather conditions, the very broken nature of the ground, and the

Sir Douglas Haig, the British Commander-in-Chief, inspects the 6th Gordon Highlanders on 15 November, 1918, four days after the signing of the Armistice.

elaborate defences encountered in the Ravine and around the village demanded more from the attackers than common resourcefulness and enterprise. Making maximum use of cover and concealment, concentrating wherever possible on points of least resistance, they advanced in small groups by a series of rushes, often taking enemy positions from flank or rear, while sustaining always the impetus of the attack. Strongpoints which could not be immediately seized were bypassed, isolated, and dealt with later by 'mopping-up' parties – usually trained bombing squads. In previous attacks, some troops had mistakenly believed that just one Mills bomb thrown down the steps of a dug-out would effectively silence the occupants, whereas in fact ten or more bombs might be needed to do the job properly. The Division was aware of this, and had arranged that one of its Battalions – the 7th Black Watch – should keep the bombers well supplied throughout the assault.

Cooperation between the participating battalions was exceptionally good within the 51st Division, and probably contributed as much as anything to its success at Beaumont

Officers of the 5th Gordon Highlanders, photographed at Armentières in August 1916. In July the battalion, forming part of General Harper's 51st Division, had suffered heavily in an assault on the notorious High Wood in the Somme area. A still more severe test awaited them at Beaumont Hamel in November 1916. 9000 Gordon Highlanders, 410 of them officers, lost their lives during the course of the War.

Hamel. Mutual support, the rapid exchange of useful information, and a willingness to come to the assistance of any hard-pressed neighbouring battalion, were always evident in the best divisions. At this stage of the War, the 51st Division was still able to fill most of the gaps in its ranks with native Scottish recruits, and there is no doubt that the bond of a shared culture contributed to the excellence of its fighting spirit. The eminent military historian Cyril Falls states that three Scottish divisions – the 9th, 15th and 51st – were 'among the best British divisions in France; some would say among the first half-dozen; some might put it even higher'.

Within a year of Beaumont Hamel the 51st Division was in fact assessed by German Military Intelligence as the most formidable in the British Army.

Taking the Empire as a whole, both friend and foe freely admitted that Canadian and Australian troops were

A group of men of the Highland Division, photographed near Bazentin-le-Petit, Somme area, in November 1916: a picture which surely illustrates the amazing resilience of the human spirit. The veteran second from the left wears a decoration for gallantry.

unsurpassed in fighting quality. The subject was carefully analysed by Peter Firkins in his book *The Australians in Nine Wars* (Hale, 1972), where he contrasted the flexible discipline and enterprising leadership seen in Dominion troops with the rigid, unimaginative attitudes of many senior British officers, and he pin-pointed the cause:

> The weakness of the British military system lay in the caste snobbery with which the entire British social system was permeated. In 1914, it was only 44 years since officers had been able to buy their commissions. Promotion was still a matter of 'who you knew' as well as 'what you knew'. Intrigue and influence, which occasionally came to the surface . . . played as much part in running the Army as did professional training and competence.

The pawns in this absurd game were of course the ordinary rank-and-file soldiers and the more junior officers:

> General Hunter-Weston's remark at Gallipoli, of 'Casualties? What do I care for casualties?' was very much a reflection of the stratification of British society; the belief that one class had been created to give orders, and another class created to

obey them – no matter what the cost might be. It was in direct contrast to the real concern shown by the Australian and other Dominion leaders for the welfare of the men under their command; a difference which was also apparent during the second World War. Apart from being lamentable in itself, the professional incompetence of a large section of the British Army leadership imposed a critical burden on the operational efficiency of that Army.

When considering a division like the 51st as it was in 1916, a distinction has to be drawn between the general term 'British' and the specific term 'Scottish'. Of course the Scots, like the English, the Welsh, and the Irish, were also 'British' troops. Unlike the Australians, they did not object when London-based newspapers wrote of their achievements as 'More British Successes in France', and they were almost reconciled to being referred to as 'English troops' by careless War Correspondents. But in fact they sometimes found that they seemed to have remarkably little in common with their English colleagues, and much more, as a rule, with men from the Dominions.

The 51st Division, for instance, was recruited largely from regions where a harsh but invigorating climate, and a Spartan mode of life, had over many generations encouraged the development of a tough, resilient, stoical breed of men; properly trained and skilfully led, such men became excellent fighting material. Like their Colonial cousins – and many Australians, Canadians and New Zealanders were Scottish in origin – these were men outspokenly scornful of the feudal practices and class distinctions which most Englishmen still tend to accept as the natural order of things. The whole idea of privilege secured by an accident of birth was to them anathema, and they gave their respect only to those who had honourably earned it. They were at that period better educated than their counterparts south of the Border, for Scottish education was then, like the Scottish Church, still a unique and influential force among its own people.

By 1916, too, the Scottish Regiments were drawing the

The Memorial at Beaumont Hamel to the officers and men of the 51st (Highland) Division who lost their lives in the 1914-18 War. A kilted Highlander looks out across Y-Ravine and the now peaceful slopes of the battlefield. On the Memorial is inscribed an old Gaelic saying: 'Là a' Bhlàir 's math na Càirdean' – 'Friends are good on the day of battle'.

bulk of their young officers not from those traditional sources, the landed gentry and sprigs of the lesser nobility, but from their own ranks: from among the thousands of teachers, farmers, businessmen, and students of the four great Scottish Universities who had answered Kitchener's summons in 1914, and who through the long months of training had shown genuine powers of leadership. Unlike so many English officers, they not only knew the social background of their men but in many cases actually shared it: thus introducing into the British Army the long-overdue concept of a leadership founded not on class but on merit.

Even with such men and such leadership, the 51st Division's attack on 13 November might still have foundered in the mud had the German military machine been what it was before 1 July. Four and a half months of continuous struggle, however, had not only shattered once and for all the German illusion of invincibility, but caused huge and irreplaceable losses in all ranks of the old, highly-trained

German Army. The capture of Beaumont Hamel, one of its strongest positions, thought by nearly everyone to be impregnable, revealed unequivocally the degree to which that Army had now deteriorated.

The 51st Division had paid lightly, in the opinion of some commentators, for its prize. The English poet and novelist, John Masefield, for example, writing to his wife in May 1917 after visiting the battlefield, observed: 'We were beaten there, with many casualties, & then we were triumphant there with hardly any . . .' On 1 July the casualties were undeniably appalling: over 5000 in the 29th Division alone. Nevertheless, is it not strange to dismiss 2200 casualties as *'hardly any'?*

Today a splendid carved figure of a kilted Highlander gazes out over Y-Ravine and the site of the battle of Beaumont Hamel; and in Scotland you may still read the names of these young men on the War Memorials of quiet villages throughout the Highlands. Their best memorial remains the memory of their valour in the minds of those of their countrymen who still cherish liberty and truth.

Further Reading

One-volume histories of the War are numerous. Some reflect too narrowly their author's special interests, or betray his prejudices and antipathies. Three which avoid such faults, and are both comprehensive and consistently fair in their judgements, are: *The First World War 1914-18* by John Terraine (Papermac, 1984); *The First World War* by Cyril Falls (Longmans, 1960); and *A Short History of World War 1* by Sir James Edmonds (Oxford University Press, 1951).

The last-named author, Sir James Edmonds, was editor-in-chief of the *History of the Great War, based on Official Documents* which was commissioned by the Committee of Imperial Defence after the War ended. Generally referred to as the *Official History*, its many volumes were written to very high standards of accuracy and impartiality, and it is unlikely to be superseded as the main work of reference for serious students. Two of its most interesting volumes, one dealing with the period August to October 1914, and the other with the period December 1915 to 1 July 1916, have recently been re-published by Shearer Publications, Woking, Surrey.

The six-volume *Official History of the War in the Air* (Oxford, 1928) describes the rôle of the Royal Flying Corps in satisfying detail; the last five volumes, edited by H.A. Jones, are particularly good. The origins and infancy of the tank are fully documented in *The Tanks* by B.H.Liddell-Hart (Cassell, 1959). The best non-specialist work on poison gases is *"Gas!"* by C.Foulkes (Blackwood, 1934). For information on the subject of military mining readers must try to obtain access to the volumes describing *The Work of the Royal Engineers in the European War* (Chatham, 1922); unfortunately these can now be found only in the larger reference libraries.

Editions of the *Encyclopaedia Britannica* which appeared

between the two world wars contained many excellent articles, often written by leading experts, on all aspects of the conflict. The articles on artillery, on machine-guns and other weapons, and on tactics are particularly worth reading. Many of these articles were removed from later editions of the *Encyclopaedia* to make room for material relating to more recent wars.

Personal memoirs of the War are so numerous as to offer an embarrassment of riches. *Liaison, 1914* by Edward Spears (Heinemann, 1930), an account of the Retreat from Mons by a young officer uniquely positioned to see the War both in close-up and in its grand perspective, is a classic. So too, though less well-known, is *The War the Infantry Knew* (King, 1938), from which the quotation at the start of Chapter 8 was taken. Paul Maze's *A Frenchman in Khaki* (Heinemann, 1934) gives an eerie description of the battlefield of Beaumont Hamel on 13 November, 1916.

Three outstanding novels about the War are *The Spanish Farm* by R.H. Mottram, *The Patriot's Progress* by Henry Williamson, and *The First Hundred Thousand* by Ian Hay. The last of those, a bestseller when it appeared in 1915, is a moving, often hilarious account by a serving officer of the moulding of a motley collection of enthusiastic Scottish volunteers into an efficient fighting unit. It would pass as a portrait of any of the battalions of the 51st (Highland) Division which fought at Beaumont Hamel.

Index